MW00640161

Unless otherwise indicated, all scripture quotations are arranged throughout the book in italics and taken from the *New King James Version* of the Bible.

You may contact D.E. Paulk at:
Spirit and Truth Sanctuary
2915 Midway Road
Decatur, GA 30030
(404) 243-5020
info@mytruthsantuary.com
www.mytruthsanctuary.com

Follow D.E. on social media:
Facebook: Donald Earl Paulk and @SpiritandTruthSanctuary
Instagram: @d.e.paulk and @spiritandtruthsanctuary
Twitter: @depaulk
YouTube: youtube.com/spiritandtruthsanctuary

FULLY AWAKE
100 Days That Will Challenge Your Mind,
Channel Your Power and Change Your Life.

Other books by D.E. Paulk:
The Holy Bible of Inclusion
I Don't Know... The Way of Knowing

Printed in the United States of America.

D.E. PAULK'S BIO

D.E. Paulk is the senior pastor of Spirit and Truth Sanctuary in Atlanta, GA, where he successfully transitioned a traditional Pentecostal Christian church into a thriving, diverse, interfaith, LGBTQ+ affirming congregation.

D.E. is widely known as radically inclusive, believes the Christ Spirit has always been present in all of creation, and cannot be defined by, nor confined to, Christianity.

> *"Descended from generations of Southern preachers, Donnie Earl is now a preacher himself, though a different breed" (Katherine Marsh, Rolling Stone Magazine, from the article Son of a Preacher Man).*
>
> *"Donnie Earl is progressive, young, hip" (Mara Shalhoup, Creative Loafing, from the article The Young Shepherd).*

In 2008, D.E. was inducted into the Dr. Martin Luther King, Jr. International Board of Preachers at Morehouse College. In 2010, he served as a board member of the Southern Christian Leadership Conference (S.C.L.C., the historic Civil Rights organization founded by Dr. Martin Luther King. Jr.), and has also served as a Dekalb County Police Chaplain.

D.E. not only serves as the senior pastor of Spirit and Truth Sanctuary, he is also the founder of the Pro-Love organization, which is an inclusive initiative purposed to bring people of all faiths, sexual identities and cultural backgrounds together. Pro-Love marches have united Christian, Muslim, Jew, Black, White, Gay, Straight and Atheist on common ground for common cause. D. E. believes this is a continuation of Dr. Martin Luther King, Jr.'s dream and a model of the "Beloved Community."

D.E. holds a Bachelor of Theology and Biblical Studies degree, is currently working on a Master of Theological Studies degree at Emory University, Candler School of Theology, and has been awarded an honorary Doctorate degree from Cornerstone University in Lake Charles, LA for his in-depth theological research and writings.

D.E. has authored eight books, including *The Holy Bible of Inclusion; I Don't Know...The Way of Knowing;* and the newly released *Fully Awake.* D. E.'s family founded Spirit and Truth Sanctuary (formerly Chapel Hill Harvester Church) in 1960. For over 60 years, Spirit and Truth has been a ministry of "Whosoever Will" and has become increasingly more inclusive and pluralistic throughout its existence.

D.E. makes his home in suburban Atlanta with his wife Brandi, and their two children, Esther and Micah.

INTRODUCTION

Most of us are not big fans of change. Yet, we all change. However, we change at our own pace and in our own space. Change is the constant. The pace of change is the variable. No one can decide our pace or choose our space for us. Some of us are capable of emptying our cups, completely surrendering our egos and experiencing change at a quantum pace. Still others of us are a bit more reluctant and connected to a particular way of thinking, doing and being. There is not one route to change or even a required speed. Life will actually tell us what our speed of change should be. How? When the pain of remaining the same becomes more painful than the pain of change…we all decide to change…and change more quickly than we might have initially planned. Pain is a very powerful teacher that doesn't need our permission or ask for our consent in order to impart wisdom or share life lessons. And, for those of us who are not blessed with mentors or guides, pain is really the only teacher any of us need.

This book is designed to bring about positive change in your experience of life. The daily affirmations, teachings and prayers are all designed to challenge and stretch you. They are not intended to break you. Over the next 100 days I am going to offer you quite a bit of food. Much of it will be inspirational. Yet, some of the teachings may feel confrontational and are purposefully designed to make you think and reconsider. Some of it will taste familiar, while some of it may be new for you. So, eat what you want and what you can. If a specific day or idea trips you up, don't eat it. You don't have to eat all of your food at one time or consume everything you are offered. When you are full…stop eating, save it for later or simply throw it out if it doesn't taste right.

Religion tells you what to think. Spirituality teaches you how to think. In other words, religion sets a plate of food in front of you and tells you to eat, and eat all of it. Spirituality invites you to a restaurant and hands you a menu. Or, presents you with a buffet of food and then allows you to decide which type of food you want and how much. This is your life, your mind and your journey. Design it to fit you. There is no grade being earned and no diploma being handed out. The reward is peace, joy and learning to channel your power while refusing to give it away any longer. Transformation is a process. So be mindful, we are after progress, not perfection.

For most of my spiritual journey I struggled with questions like: "Is this accurate?" "Am I right or wrong?" "Who is correct?" These questions can never really be fully answered because life is not an exact science, or a "one size fits all" and radically varies from one perspective, one person and one place to another. What works for me may be destructive for you. Freedom may be the life giving element for one individual while freedom for others would quickly land them in bondage and enslavement.

The only question that really matters in life is this: IS IT WORKING FOR ME? All other questions are only feeding the ego, distracting from the real work that needs to be done and wasting valuable time and precious energy. Questions of right and wrong and arguments of accurate and inaccurate must all yield and give way to the truth of what works. And, what is working for one person may not be what works for another. Further, what worked for us during one leg of our journey may not work for us now. Consider each lesson. Ponder each idea. Chew on each bite. "Rightly divide the Word of Truth." Trust the Spirit of God within you to discern what is healthy for you, and what might be harmful. Let's walk together as we Challenge our Minds, Channel our Power, Change our Lives…and become Fully Awake!

A SUGGESTION

For each day of this journey, I want to encourage you to recite this Prayer of Surrender before you begin your daily affirmation and teaching. This is a simple invitation of truth that sets up the conditions for your soul to be fed and prepares the ground of your mind to be open and available for transformation.

PRAYER OF SURRENDER

> "Spirit of Truth, CARRY ME where You will, BRING TO ME what You will, TAKE FROM ME what You will, AWAKEN IN ME what You will. The Christ MAN is AROUND me. The Christ MIND is IN me. The Christ POWER flows THROUGH me. And, the Christ MYSTERY exists AS me. I believe it. I perceive it. And, now I receive it! I am surrendered. Amen."

Today I will challenge my mind, Channel my power and change my life

100 AFFIRMATIONS

Day 1 - Say It. See It. Survey It. Shift It.
Day 2 - Healthy Religion
Day 3 - A Righteous Fast
Day 4 - Generational Curses or Blessings?
Day 5 - Don't Ask Declare
Day 6 - Renewing My Mind
Day 7 - Created, Creative, Creating
Day 8 - Pay It Forward
Day 9 - Attitude, Aptitude and Altitude
Day 10 - Victim? Or Victor?
Day 11 - Choose Peace. Seek Peace. Pursue Peace.
Day 12 - The Senility Prayer
Day 13 - Single-Minded and Stable
Day 14 - A Flexible Faith
Day 15 - My Body Is A Temple
Day 16 - 7 Universal Timeless Truths
Day 17 - A Vision of Love
Day 18 - The Name of God
Day 19 - The Divine Observer
Day 20 - Change Is the Only Constant
Day 21 - Living Above the Political Divide
Day 22 - Behind The Scenes
Day 23 - No Weapon
Day 24 - Honoring Our Ancestors
Day 25 - Room to Grow
Day 26 - The Way of Jesus
Day 27 - Let Me Be Spiritual
Day 28 - Protected By An Enemy
Day 29 - The Same… Yesterday, Today and Forever
Day 30 - The Speck and The Plank
Day 31 - Creating God In My Image
Day 32 - The Beginner's Mind
Day 33 - The Pee-Pee Prayer

Excerpts and previews of D.E. Paulk's other books included...

FULLY AWAKE

100 Days That Will Challenge Your Mind, Channel Your Power and Change Your Life.

D. E. Paulk

Day 1

Say It. See It. Survey It. Shift It.

Affirmation

> *"My greatest gift is that I am created in the image and likeness of God (and good). This means, I am Created BY God…Creative LIKE God…and Creating AS a god. I am finally willing to stir up the gift of divine image and god-likeness within me. As I embrace my God-given divinity, I will awaken to my full power and potential. God SAID it. God SAW it. God SURVEYED it. Today, I will harness my full power as I SAY it, SEE it and SURVEY it!"*

In the very first chapter of the Bible, we find a beautiful pattern of divine creativity. God said, *"let there be light."* Then God saw what He said. Then God surveyed what He saw (*"said that it was good"*). The divine pattern we discover is: First, Say it. Next, See it. Then, Survey it. This is a textbook example of responsible creativity. As divine creatures, created in the image and likeness of the Divine Creator, we must learn to create in the same way. We create by speaking. Then, we will eventually see what we have spoken. And hopefully, we will have the honesty and objectivity to survey what we have spoken and created.

What happens when we don't like what we survey? If (and that's a BIG IF) we have the courage to own what we have created, we have the ability to shift it…or re-create it. When God created man, we see the same pattern: God said it. God saw it. God surveyed it. But, this time, God saw that man was alone. God surveyed that this was not good. So, God created again (a companion) or shifted it. We have the same power! We can re-create our lives whenever we have the strength to own what we create and then create something new, something that brings peace, love and joy into our daily experience. This is the process of taking responsibility for our divine creativity. Or to make it plain, this is how we take responsibility for our lives and the experience of life we are creating.

> **Prayer:** *"Creative Word, give me the wisdom to SAY IT, the courage to SEE IT, the honesty to SURVEY IT and the strength to SHIFT IT. Amen."*

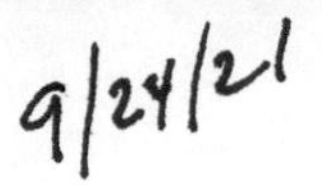

Healthy Religion

Affirmation

"Today, I set my intention to practice Healthy Religion. The hurt caused by my past religious experiences and expressions can serve to open my eyes to a bigger and better vision and version of the awesomeness of God, and of me! If fear, shame, intolerance and inflexibility have not produced a harvest peace, joy and love in my life, I am willing to let go of unhealthy thoughts and unhealthy religion. I have received new wine. I will not put it into an old wineskin. Today I will begin the journey of creating a healthy religion, healthy mind, healthy thoughts, healthy body and healthy relationships."

In almost 30 years of full time ministry I have heard countless stories of how positive, and negative, the effects of religion have been on many people's lives. I have encountered amazing stories of the beauty of worship and God's presence. Conversely, I have endured tearful accounts of condemnation and manipulation in the name of God.

The tendency is to either buy it all or reject it all. So many people hold to the idea that it's either all true or it's all a lie. In my study of all the major world religions I have discovered profound truth and also uncovered ridiculous fallacies. I have been overwhelmed with timeless wisdom and been shocked by cultural craziness. There is an old saying, "Don't throw the baby out with the bathwater." Seek to find a healthy balance where you are open to truth contained in religion, but also vigilant and watchful not to be deceived by man's devising.

Prayer: *"Eternal God, today I purpose in my heart to practice healthy religion. I have been helped and hurt by religion. My soul is thirsty for a path that cultivates a spiritual awakening and an ever-expanding consciousness. Grant me the wisdom to receive what is healthy for me. And, bless me with discernment to know what is harmful. Amen!"*

Day 3

9/25/2021

A Righteous Fast

Affirmation

"God takes no pleasure in my suffering. God takes delight in my prosperity. God does not need to see me in pain in order for me to prove the depth of my love or the level of my commitment. I am capable of shifting my paradigm about fasting. I am not anointed NOT TO DO. I am appointed TO DO! I will not live a life founded on what I keep from doing. I will spend my energy focusing on what I can do. I will create joy. I will pursue peace. I will heal the hurting. I will be inclusive of those who have been left out. This week, I will be conscious of the truth that what I DO is so much more powerful than what I DON'T DO!"

Just Do It!

I grew up around the discipline of fasting... fasting food, chocolate, soda, meat, television, radio. We fasted 40 days during Lenten and then every Friday of the year. We fasted when we wanted God to answer a prayer, change His mind or share His mind with us. I used to think many of our church members fasted smiling and laughing because they were so serious all the time...especially when fasting! Fasting was just a vital part of my religious experience and expression. Somehow we believed that suffering would get God's attention or at least prove to God how much we loved Him.

My tradition's fasting consciousness subtly conditioned us to believe God enjoyed our pain and suffering. Consequently, we focused more on what we couldn't do than on what we could do or should be doing. The prophet Isaiah gives us a beautiful alternative to religion's traditional view of fasting (Isaiah 58:6-7). Isaiah instructs us to DO something, not keep from doing something. Set the oppressed free. Feed the hungry. Include the outcast. This is the fast God has ordained. Ironically, Isaiah tells us to fast fasting.

Prayer: *"Spirit of Truth, today I will begin a new fast. Empower me to help others by what I DO...not by what I keep from doing. I know You are more pleased when I love my neighbor than when I starve myself. Today, I choose the fast You have ordained. Amen."*

9/26/2024

Generational Curses or Blessings?

8/12/21

Affirmation

"Generational curses have no power over me or my family. I will not be a victim of any former generation's choices. I am the BREAKER of bad choices, harmful cultures or negative cycles. Today, I choose life and blessing! Today, I create righteousness, joy and peace to be passed down to the next generation."

There is actually no such thing as a generational curse. On the surface, it may look like a curse that has been passed down for generations. However, as we dig deeper we discover that it isn't a curse at all. Generational cycles exist from generational cultures and customs that are the result of generational choices.

Contrary to popular belief and faddish preaching, God does not play favorites. God doesn't favor Jacob over Esau. God doesn't bless Isaac and curse Ishmael. The "curse of Ham" has not been passed down to people of color throughout generations. We are not helpless victims.
We are powerful victors!

There may be a cycle in your family that has been accepted as a way of life for generations. Yet, you can change this cycle and choose a different experience of life by simply making different choices. You are the creation of a creative Creator and you carry the same divine DNA. What does this mean? Your Creator gave you the power to create! So, wake up to who you are and stop giving your power away to any idea of being the victim of an unbreakable family curse. Create the life you want to experience by making good choices that become powerful customs that create healthy cycles that yield positive cultures. You can do it!

Prayer: *"Heavenly Father, thank you for gifting me with the power to choose, change and create. I give thanks that I am blessed, not cursed. Today, I pass down blessings to generations who come after me. Amen."*

Create choices, customs, healthy cycles yielding positive cultures!

Don't Ask... Declare!

9/29/21

Affirmation

> *"Today, I will not ask. I will declare! I will not speak that I lack anything. On the converse, I will give thanks in advance! Instead of asking for anything, I will be open and available for Spirit to reveal to me what I already have."*

Asking for something is a very subtle admission that you don't have it. This is why Jesus said, *"when you pray, believe you already have what you're asking for"* (Mark 11:24). God does not desire to be begged for anything. God especially doesn't want us to grab onto the horns of the altar and refuse to let go until we somehow successfully persuade God by relentless begging and graveling. God takes pleasure in our prosperity. God's desire is to give us the kingdom. God wants us to have long life. Furthermore, God has already *"given us all things pertaining to life"* (2 Peter 1:3). Why would we ask for something we already have?

So, our approach must line up with these powerful truths. We must awaken to the revelation that we can approach the throne of grace boldly. King Solomon shares some wisdom with us that *"as we think, so are we"* (Proverbs 23:7). If we perceive we are lacking, then that is what we will create. We must begin to speak from power, being confident that God is good, that all good flows from God and that God would not keep any good thing from us. Instead of asking for something and making a declaration of lack, declare that you already have it. If you ask for anything simply ask that God reveal to you what you already have.

Jesus trusts us with a powerful truth. We don't have to ask for anything. All we must do is *"seek first the Kingdom of God, and all these things will be added to us"* (Matthew 6:33).

> ***Prayer:*** *"Divine Creator, today I give thanks that I have all things pertaining to life and that I need not ask or beg for anything. I only ask that You allow me to see what You have already given to me. Amen."*

RenewING My Mind

Affirmation

"Today, I agree to the renewING of my mind...which is a constant and ongoing process. Faith comes by hearING, not by having heard. Similarly, I am transformed by the renewING of my mind, and not by any renewED mind or mindset. I am an eternal spirit having a temporary earthly experience and fleeting human expression."

"*Faith comes by hearing...*" (Romans 10:17). On the surface this seems simple. All we have to do is listen to the words of the Bible being taught and we will have faith. However, on a deeper level, faith (or faith-ing) is the result of an ongoing process of continually hearing. The ING on the word hearING suggests this may not be a one-time thing. Just two chapters later we stumble across this ING principle again – "*be transformed by the renewing of your mind*" (Romans 12:2). The transformation happens, not from a renewed mind, but from a renewING of the mind.

Jesus struggled to teach this ING principle to the Pharisees and religious order of His day. He often said to them "*you have heard of old, but I say.*" In other words, you are living in the past and I am speaking to you now. Your faith has been stunted because you exist on what you heard, what you read or what was said. They struggled to live in the present moment...in the hearing, the saying, the renewing. When it comes to spiritual growth, one of the most detrimental habits hindering expansion is living in the past while attempting to create the present. Jesus gives us a clue when He taught that "*man should not live by bread alone but by every word that proceeds from the mouth of God.*" In other words, God is still speaking. Are you hearing?

Prayer: *"Holy Spirit, I set my intention for hearing and renewing. I am available for a fresh daily bread and an organic living word from You. I surrender to the truth that I cannot live organically in spirit while eating only religious preservatives and leftovers. Amen."*

Created, Creative and Creating

Affirmation

> *"I am created BY God. I am creative LIKE God. And, I am creating AS a god. I am awake to the truth that life is not happening to me or around me. I am a created, creative and creating divine being and life is happening THROUGH ME and AS ME!"*

In the first chapter of Genesis (1:27), we find possibly the most powerful truth in the entire Bible…we are created like God! This verse records, *"Let Us make man in Our image and according to Our likeness."* Then, we find out in the next chapter that mankind is commissioned to begin using this divine creativity. Adam begins the process of creating his reality by naming the animals, tending the ground, making choices…learning to use and navigate his God given power to create. It sounds strange to the religious ear, but we are walking divinities. If you will, we are little gods. Jesus attempted to explain this to the Pharisees when He quoted Psalm 98 reminding them, *"you are all gods."* Their response wasn't very accepting. They wanted to stone Him for this perceived blasphemy.

Why is it important to awaken to this revelation of being created like God? Sadly, until we get this truth we will remain powerless victims relying on power-stealing doctrines of chance and leaning on victimizing theologies of favor. When you know that you are created by God, creative like God and creating as a god, you begin to wake up to this truth…you can create the life you want to experience…today! No waiting on God, wishing for a blessing or wanting a new season. No devil can keep you from it and no pastor can prophesy you into it. You have a God given power to create. Use it!

> **Prayer:** *"Creator of the Universe, Thank you for the blessing of divine creativity. I am grateful and amazed You imparted into me a piece of You. Open my eyes and let me see just how powerful I really am. Give me strength to manifest love and create peace. Enable me with courage to be daring enough to use the greatest gift You gave to me…You! Amen."*

8/16/21

Pay It Forward

9/30/2021

Affirmation

"Today, I choose to Pay It Forward to others and to my future self. Future generations, and the future Me, depend on the seeds I plant today. As I Pay It Forward to others, I am also investing into myself, as I am interconnected to all of the human family. As Christ Paid It Forward to me, I will Pay It Forward to every child of God! Amen."

To Pay It Forward means to do a good deed for someone today knowing that in the process of sowing and reaping, action and reaction, or karma… that good deed will continue to be paid forward to others and eventually find its way back to you. Or perhaps, someone already paid it forward to you and you are simply paying it forward to someone else with gratitude. In a sense, when you bless someone else you are blessing yourself. Dr. Martin Luther King, Jr. once declared that we are all intrinsically connected in an inescapable web of mutuality… *"what affects one directly, affects us all indirectly…injustice anywhere is a threat to justice everywhere."*

My son was playing in his first college basketball game in Kentucky. This particular college arena had an enormous picture on one of the walls of identical twin brothers running a relay race. One twin was handing the baton off to the other twin. It looked as if the same person was handing something to himself. In essence, that's what we do every day. We pay it forward to our future selves by the choices we make today. We sow seeds of love and inclusion and kindness that impact someone somewhere and make the world a better place to inhabit. And, when the world around us is more loving, we reap the harvest.

Prayer: *"Magnificent Mother, I am overwhelmed by what You have freely given to me. As I bless others, I am paying it forward with a heart of thanksgiving. And, I am paying it forward to my future self. Grant me an opportunity today to Pay It Forward in some way. Amen."*

Attitude, Aptitude and Altitude

Affirmation

> *"My attitude, not just my aptitude, determines my altitude. I will protect my inner kingdom by maintaining my joy and by keeping my peace. No one can change my attitude but me. This week I will fly above the storm of worry and rise above the turbulence of anxiety. I will learn to let it go. I will raise the vibration of those around me by maintaining mine!"*

I have often been amazed that the most successful people I have either met or studied are not always the most qualified. Many times these powerful leaders don't possess a high level of aptitude. However, they own a contagious positive attitude. The result is they reach great heights of altitude. My wife is a CPA and has worked for several Fortune 500 companies. During the interview process, she has discovered that the most qualified person doesn't always land the job. Many times the candidate hired is actually the most likeable, and carries an attitude that helps to foster a positive, productive and peaceful work environment.

Unfortunately, there are times when a person's qualifications disqualify them as they carry with them a "know it all" attitude. They smugly allow their higher aptitude to place them into a lower altitude. How many great athletes never reached the professional ranks because they were un-coachable? How many phenomenal musicians never reached their potential because no one could tolerate working with them? There is a healthy balance of being knowledgeable without becoming "a know it all."

There is an old church cliché, "God doesn't always call the qualified. Sometimes, God qualifies the called." We need to be qualified. But, more importantly, we need to maintain the right spirit.

Prayer: *"Mind of the Universe, I am willing to study, prepare and apply myself to acquire knowledge. As You grant me knowledge, I humbly ask for a spirit of wisdom in how to use this knowledge. Amen."*

Day 10

Victim? Or Victor?

Affirmation

"I am not a victim. I am a victor! I am not bitter. I am better! I am not what people call me. I am what I answer to. Your 'YOU ARE' will never be as powerful as my 'I AM!' Today, I will only answer to righteousness, peace and joy."

The first name we have for God in the Bible is simply *"I Am."* God begins a conversation with Moses and instructs him to go speak certain things to a very powerful Pharaoh. Moses asks God, *"who should I say sent me?"* God replies, *"tell them I Am that I Am sent you."* Seems awfully vague and abstract. Doesn't it? Yet, this is possibly the most brilliant answer ever given. God would not say a specific name because that would be a limiting decision. *"I Am that I Am"* leaves an entire universe open to possibilities. In other words, I am not what you say I am. I Am who I say I Am! A wise man once told me "Once people can define you they will disqualify you."

Many people in our lives use the two words "you are" to describe what they think of us. Nevertheless, "you are" has absolutely no power over us. The power is in the "I Am!" The only way "you are" impacts us is if we allow someone else's "you are" to become our "I am." Never allow anyone's "you are" to become your "I Am!"

Only what you say after "I am" really matters. I am not a victim of anything that anyone has done to me. I am a victor who has overcome. I am not a survivor. I am thriving and what didn't kill me made me stronger. What didn't break me made more flexible. And, my mistakes have only made me wiser.

Prayer: *"Infinite I Am that I Am, I give thanks today that my 'I am' is stronger than anyone's 'you are.' I am grateful that life and death are in the power of my tongue…not anyone else's. Grant me the strength today to speak from the power of I am. Amen."*

Day 11

Choose Peace. Seek Peace. Pursue Peace.

Affirmation

"Today I choose peace by seeking it and pursuing it. I acknowledge I am an active participant in creating my peace and not a helpless victim waiting for someone to speak peace to me or create peace for me. I will maintain a high vibration by avoiding lower vibrations (and crazy people) whenever possible. I am aware that seeking revenge and harboring unhealthy thoughts can transform me into the thing I resent. I am not the thing that happened to me and I will not smell like it for the rest of my life. I am aware that peace is not the absence of chaos as I can choose to create peace in the midst of a storm. My mind is clear. My heart is healthy. And, my life will reflect my thoughts! In this moment, I choose peace!"

The Bible instructs us to *"Seek peace and pursue it" (Psalm 34:14 / 1 Peter 3:11)*. Interesting verbs…seek and pursue. These are not passive words. To seek for something is literally to *go on a quest…searching.* To pursue means *striving to gain.* With this understanding we can surmise that peace is not something that happens by accident. Peace does not fall into our laps or leisurely stroll into our lives. Peace doesn't happen by chance. Peace happens by choice!

How do we choose peace? There are many ways we can choose peace every day. One way we choose peace is by being aware that peace is not the absence of chaos. Life is stressful, complicated, tense. No surprise. So, peace must be a premeditated choice. Mentally choose peace in advance of any situation or conversation that could potentially steal your peace. Choose your vibration and don't allow anyone to lower it. Fly above the turbulence by maintaining a great attitude. Seek Peace. Pursue peace!

Prayer: *"God of peace, I know that You will keep me in perfect peace as I choose, seek and pursue peace. Whatever storm or drama I am in will never be in me. The world didn't give me peace and the world can't take it away. Today, I am at peace as I maintain and keep my peace. Empower me to keep my peace by not giving it away. Amen."*

Day 12

The Senility Prayer

Affirmation

"God, grant me the senility to forget the people I never liked anyway, the good fortune to run into the ones that I do, and the eyesight to tell the difference."

Most people have heard of the Serenity Prayer. Have you ever experienced the Senility Prayer? Although it is obviously humorous, there is an amazing amount of wisdom in this silly prayer. Jesus said *"Agree quickly with your adversary while you are in the way with him" (Matthew 5:25).* Jesus and Luke give us a great avoidance plan that when someone doesn't like you or accept you, simply stay away from them and *"shake the dust off your feet" (Matthew 10:14; Mark 6:11; Luke 9:5; Acts 13:51).*

One of the most painful lessons of adolescence is when we learn that everyone is not our friend. To say it positively, all of us will eventually find our tribe. How many years have we wasted trying to fit in with a certain crowd or win a specific person over? Eventually, either by frustration, exhaustion, or by default, we shake the dust of rejection off of our feet and move on to a place or acceptance and inclusion.

Similar to society, the Body of Christ is made up of many different parts and expressions. I don't have to hang out with the parts that are not on my vibratory level to appreciate that this diversity brings about a necessary balance. Many people are born into families that don't understand or celebrate them. As much as they strive for approval and affirmation it may never happen. For survival, they may have to remain in an environment of tolerance until they are self-sufficient. Inevitably, the day will come when they will choose to be celebrated, not tolerated. Maybe this is that day?

Prayer: *"God of Wisdom, in my heart I know I deserve to be loved and accepted. Give me the strength to walk toward celebration and away from toleration. Amen."*

10/5/2021

8/21/2021

Single-Minded and Stable

Affirmation

"I know that a double minded man is unstable is in all of his ways! There is no duality in this universe; there is only ONE power...ONE God...ONE Mind. And, that power is working IN, THROUGH, AROUND, FOR and AS me! I will own my creation and allow irritating people and situations to be the spiritual sandpaper smoothing my rough edges."

I grew up on a steady diet of "devilology." That is to say, my church and religious experience was founded on the devil as much as it was on God or Jesus. The devil seemed to somehow be responsible for every bad thing that grown adults consciously created. Financial irresponsibility, relationship failures, unruly teenagers, unfaithful spouses, mechanical problems, inclement weather, political turbulence...everything was to be blamed on the devil and attributed to spiritual warfare or some invisible battle happening in the unseen world.

Far be it for me to take anyone's devil away from them. My goal is not to eliminate the devil - it is to empower people. And, we cannot tap into our God-given strength while giving all of our power away. The best way to become powerful is by not giving it away. When we attribute our own poor choices to a devil or anything other than ourselves, we are subtly, and perhaps even subconsciously, throwing our creative capacity in the trash.

Believe in the devil. Don't believe in the devil. That's your own spiritual journey. If it's working for you, work it. However, double mindedness and devil blaming leads to instability and powerlessness. Own your creation. Wake up to your power. Rest in the truth that all creativity comes from God.

Prayer: *"One Power of the Universe, grant unto me stability and single-mindedness. I know all things were created by You, for You and exist in You. Give me wisdom in what to create and courage to own it. Amen."*

10/4/2021

8/24/21

A Flexible Faith

Affirmation

"My faith is NOT fragile. My faith is FLEXIBLE. I am willing to shift so that I will not be shattered. Religion breeds rigidity. And, rigidity breeds weakness. I am NOT religious, rigid or weak! I am flexible, strong, open and available for Spirit to guide me into all truth. As I journey from glory to glory, I will keep an open mind and maintain a young spirit."

One of my favorite preachers would say, "Blessed are the flexible, for they shall not be broken." How powerful! Strength lies in flexibility, not in rigidity. The tallest skyscrapers are designed to sway with the wind so they don't collapse and crumble. Only the trees that bend in a heavy storm survive. Can this principle of flexibility be applied to our spiritual lives? "Mighty fortresses," "strong towers," "solid rocks" are fairly common lyrics and phrases in the religious world. Strength seems to always be parallel with a rigid regimen of changelessness. Yet, we are encouraged to go from glory to glory; to advance from one precept to another precept; to be changed, renewed, transformed. God feeds us with manna (mystery), Daily Bread (daily word), Living Water (organic spirituality), Living Wells (new avenues) and Green Pastures (fresh places). Organic spirituality demands flexibility and openness. Perhaps this is why Jesus repeatedly said *"you have heard of old, but I say"* as a challenge to those who were stuck in a religious rut?

Jesus spent a great deal of His ministry dealing with religious rigidity. Unbending, unopen, unteachable religious orders of sincere men who lacked flexibility of mind. Jesus is so complex and challenging that rigidity of thought will inevitably lead to theological crisis. In order to follow Jesus, and be led by the Holy Spirit into new truth, there must be a flexibility of thought and openness to progress. Resistance and rigidity will only detour us directly to ignorance, irrelevance, denial…and eventually to collapse.

Prayer: *"God of Strength, empower me to bend and not break; shift and not be shattered; to sway, grow, unfold and evolve. Amen."*

Day 15

10/7/2021

8/23/2021

My Body is a Temple

Affirmation

"Today, I am aware that my body is the temple of the Holy Spirit. This temporary physical body houses my eternal spiritual self and soul. My physical body temple may not last forever. However, while I am in it, I will honor and respect it while it helps to facilitate my purpose and impact on the world and on those around me. Today, I choose to be aware of both unhealthy patterns and healthy alternatives. Today, I choose divine health over divine healing. Today, I choose to do my part in creating a long, happy and healthy life."

Healing evangelists and miracle services were not uncommon in the church where I was raised. Occasionally, I did witness some divine moments of healing taking place for others and even in myself. In this atmosphere and culture of the miraculous I noticed a subtle, dangerous line of thinking. I watched as many sincere believers began leaning toward divine healing, not divine health. I observed levelheaded, good-hearted people choose a practice of treatment rather than creating a pattern of prevention. To be plain, I watched people neglect their physical health and then ask God to heal them when their bodies reacted to this poor treatment.

I believe in divine healing and in God's power! But, I also believe we have a responsibility to care for our body temples and respect its function of carrying our spirits and facilitating our earthly purposes. All of us are genetically predisposed both to certain physical strengths and health risks. We may not be able to change our genetic codes. Yet, we can do the best with what we are given. Make the choice today to exercise, eat, rest and live in such a way that your physical body temple will fulfill its destiny of carrying your spirit until it makes its transition back to God.

Prayer: *"Divine Healer, give me the discipline to choose divine health. Empower me to respect my body as the temple of the Holy Spirit. Fill my stomach with healthy food and my mind with healthy thoughts. Amen."*

Day 16

7 Universal Timeless Truths

Affirmation

"God is within…not up there, out there, on the way or in the past. I can experience God and live in the Kingdom right now. Healthy religion is simple and universal: Love God, love your neighbor as you love yourself. The reason this is not effective is because it is backwards. I must learn to love myself, then I will be able to love my neighbor, then I will understand how to love God. I will fill my consciousness with good thoughts and be conscious that I am eternally a created, creative and creating being. As I think in my heart, so am I. I will not give my power away or my mind over to any religious leader, pastor, guru or teacher. I give thanks for them all. But, the Holy Spirit will always be the most important Teacher in my life. For the rest of my life, I will rightly divide the Word of Truth…rightly divide my pastors…and rightly divide myself. I am healthy, happy and whole! And, with this new wineskin, I am now empowered to remain this way!"

1. **God is within me** (not up there, out there, on the way or in the past).
2. **Love God, neighbor and myself** (but in reverse order).
3. **Be aware of my Spirit** (prayer, worship, meditate, study, be in service to others).
4. **Fill my temple with good thoughts** (your life is a reflection of your thoughts. Put good in and get good out).
5. **I am Created BY God, Creative LIKE God and Creating AS a god** (I am created in the image and likeness of a Divine Creator and I am creating).
6. **No religious leader should control my life or destroy my faith** (I will respect spiritual guides but never allow them full control of my journey).
7. **If I am not experiencing Righteousness, Peace and Joy I must reexamine my spiritual practice** (nothing else needs to be said)!

Prayer: *"Indwelling Spirit, etch these timeless truths onto my heart and into my consciousness. Lead me into a healthy spiritual practice and into a pattern of growth and fulfillment. Holy Spirit, guide me into all truth. Amen."*

Day 17

8/20/2021 10/9/2021

A Vision of Love

Affirmation

"Today, I bring all of me to God...I bring my pain and my past, my filters and my frustrations, my lenses and my losses. As I bring them all out, I know I will be able to see them more clearly. On this day, I choose to see them and not see life through them! On this day, I choose to create my life through the Vision of Love and not through any filter of pain. Bad things have happened to me. However, I am not the things that have happened to me! I am an eternal Spirit having a temporary human experience."

In 1990 Mariah Carey exploded onto the music scene with her hit song "Vision of Love." I can remember the first time I heard her voice. Like most of the world, I was captivated and moved. One line in this song still resonates with me: "I visualized the love that came to be." What a powerful truth. Things that come to be are visualized first. This principle works both positively and negatively. Most of us have had an experience in our past that caused us a tremendous amount of pain and sorrow. When the event, loss, relationship, sickness is finally over, we are shocked to see this very thing show up in our lives again and again. This is not a simple matter of bad luck, a curse, being snake-bitten or the devil being "busy." We subconsciously create our future experiences using filters of past hurts. Fear, jealousy, pessimism, suspicion, superstition all help to create a filter through which we see the world and unknowingly manifest our reality.

Let go of the past and any lingering filters hanging around in the back of your subconscious mind. You are not the thing that happened to you. What didn't kill you made you stronger. What didn't break you taught you how to bend. Your past failures are now your present wisdom. Consciously choose to see and create life through a new Vision of Love, not an old filter of pain. Today is a new day. Visualize love and watch it come to be!

Prayer: *"God of Vision, remove any filter of pain and give me a vision of love. Empower me to visualize and then create love, peace and joy. Amen."*

The Name of God

Affirmation

"I will not allow my individual religious beliefs to further separate the corporate human family. The name I call God is not God's name…it is just one of many names humans use in an attempt to name the unnamable; define the undefinable; describe the indescribable, eternal, I Am that I Am! Today, I will neither curse the darkness nor unconsciously add to it. Instead, I will consciously create righteousness, peace and joy by allowing the light and love within me to be manifested all around me! Amen."

According to the Bible, before the erecting of the Tower of Babel, the earth and all of its inhabitants spoke one common language (Genesis 11). We can assume this means there was one universal name for God. Thus, there was no need to argue over the name of God. In early Hebrew law, even saying the name of God was forbidden. Personally, I don't believe God wanted His/Her name to be so revered that no one should dare utter it. I choose to believe that God knew having different names, spoken by diverse languages, would cause division among His children. When Moses finally asks God *"what is Your name?"* (Exodus 3) God continues to remain nameless, or at least refuses to offer Moses a specific name. Instead, God simply answers *"I AM WHO I AM."* In other words, God is attempting to express to Moses that He is more of an essence than a definable name.

How can the global human family be so divided over the name(s) of God? Yahweh, Jesus, Buddha, Zeus, Krishna, Allah… all human names for God and strong points of disagreement and disunity. I believe the segregation that began at Babel was reversed on the Day of Pentecost when the Holy Spirit enabled people of different languages and cultures to understand each other. When we choose to speak in Spirit, not in religion, we will be able to connect with every person we encounter, regardless of their religion, language or name for God.

Prayer: *"Lord, make me an instrument of Your peace. Amen."*

Day 19

8/28/2021 10/11/2021

The Divine Observer

Affirmation

"I am not getting older. I am growing wiser! I am not broke. I am learning to be faithful over a little as God is making me ruler over much! I am not lonely. I am learning to love myself! I have never failed at anything, but I have started over again many times with more wisdom! I am not a sinner or sinning. I am only learning how to navigate my Innate God-given Divine Creativity. And, I can re-create my life anytime I desire a new existence. I am not my experiences. I am the Divine Observer of these experiences."

We chose to come here, to earth, from a spiritual dimension, to experience temporary situations and even painful difficulties, for the evolution of our eternal spirits. This mystical idea is beginning to gain quite a bit of popularity in many circles. Whether it is true or not…I really can't say. I am learning that I don't necessarily believe everything I consider. However, if there is something of truth or even anything helpful, I will continue to consider it as long as it brings me to a higher awareness of my divine self and soul. The Bible speaks of God knowing us before we were formed in our mother's wombs. Jesus, chose to come to earth for a higher purpose. Scripture speaks of us being predestined for a purpose and that certain good works were already put in place for us "beforehand."

If this idea is true, then when bad things happen to us or even through us, we can step away from the event itself, and look at it as a Divine Observer. In this context, the event happening "to us" is not personal or even permanent. It is designed to teach us or help us learn how to better navigate our Divine Creativity to manifest the reality we desire to experience. Can you step back from past experiences and see the learning without being overwhelmed by the pain? Try it. You might outgrow the pain.

Prayer: *"God before time, I am not what happens to me. Today, I declare nothing has or is happening TO ME. All life is happening THROUGH ME, FOR ME and AS ME! I am here to observe, grow, evolve and create. Amen."*

Day 20

Change is the Only Constant

Affirmation

"Change is the only constant in my life. As my divinity continues to unfold I will progress from one season to the next. Friends will come and go. And, as they do, I will not live in bitterness or un-forgiveness. On the contrary, I will remain open and give thanks for each new level of understanding and the newness it brings. I am not what I have, do, believe or what others think of me. I am..."

Change is the only constant in the universe. The universe continues to expand. Animals, and humans, continue to evolve and adapt. And, our ideas, philosophies, theologies, opinions and perspectives will change until the moment we make our transition back to Spirit. As we continually change, we will make new friends and lose touch with old friends. One of my mentors told me that every person only gets five lifetime friends. I don't believe this means we are all negligent and unfaithful as friends. On a deeper level, we are all unfolding and growing spiritually at our own pace and in our own space. When one friend's growth or pace of change is slower, there will be a natural distancing. We are all vibrational beings in a vibrational universe. When our vibration no longer matches the vibration of our friends, there will be an unseen force pushing us away from some friends and attracting others to us who share our same vibration. This is not just spiritual. Scientifically, this is an understanding of magnetism.

With this knowledge, we can feel less bitter about friends failing to keep in touch and also feel better about not keeping in touch with old friends. It is not simply that "life happens." Change and vibration happen. Bless people as they vibrate away and leave your life. Welcome new friends as they vibrate toward and are attracted to you. This way, you keep your mind open to new growth and your heart free from bitterness.

Prayer: *"Original Vibration, I am awake to the laws of attracting to and vibrating away. I release what goes and welcome what comes. Amen."*

Day 21

Living Above the Political Divide

Affirmation

> *"Whether I call myself a Democrat, Republican, Liberal or Conservative, I can find biblical backing to support my particular political platform. My political views are not necessarily the politics of Jesus nor are they the official platform for political Christianity. My political views are mine and they are evolving. I am not my political views or my religious beliefs. I am an eternal Spirit capable of having and changing temporary opinions. As a peacemaker, this week I will endeavor to find a way to bring people together, not cause further division."*

Jesus taught that a rich man could not enter the Kingdom. He also instructed that if we don't receive interest on our investments, we will be cast into outer darkness (parable of the talents). Jesus told the rich young ruler to sell everything and give the money to the poor. He also rebuked Judas (wanting to sell an expensive fragrance and give the proceeds to the poor) by saying *"the poor you have with you always."* Jesus scourged Peter for using a sword and then later told the disciples to sell everything and buy some swords. It would be inaccurate to make Jesus a Democrat or a Republican. He seemed to vacillate between the two political platforms. Similarly, Paul taught the early church to *"hold all things (possessions) in common."* Paul also instructed that if *"a person doesn't work they don't eat."* Who knew Paul was both a Socialist and a Conservative?

What is the purpose of this? To encourage all followers of Christ to cease from using the Bible, or Jesus, as political weapons to support their particular political platform. The Bible and its teachings are complex, and at times contradictory. Instead of focusing on a few verses to promote a candidate or cause, why not focus on verses that foster unity and help to fill the chasm created by Christians misusing scripture for political gain.

Prayer: *"Father, make us one. Help us focus on our commonalities. Use me as an advocate for peace, not a pawn for politics. Amen."*

10/14/21

8/31/21

Behind the Scenes

Affirmation

"Today, I am aware that God's ways are higher than my ways. I cannot always see what's going on behind the scenes. However, I trust that all things are working together for my good and that I will understand God's plan someday. Until then, I will be of a good report, meditate on positive thoughts and maintain a high vibration. It's all good and all God!"

Whether we are facing a worldwide pandemic like the Coronavirus or struggling through the pain of losing a loved one, all of us have experienced moments where we are left searching for answers. Imagine Joshua's dilemma, being told by God to march around the walls of Jericho (without weapons) playing trumpets and praising God until the walls collapse. Put yourself in Gideon's shoes as he is facing an army of 300,000 men. God tells him all he needs is 300 weaponless men, running around and making noise with lanterns. Consider Moses being commissioned by God to tell Pharaoh *"let My people go"* and then God hardening Pharaoh's heart so that he wouldn't let the people go. Wouldn't it be nice to get a glimpse behind the scenes and into the mind of God?

In Isaiah 45:7 we get a little peek behind the scenes… *"I form the light and create darkness, I make peace and create calamity; I, the Lord, do all these things."* God can and does use what we perceive as evil for good! The walls of Jericho fell. Gideon won the war. Moses and the children of Israel escaped the bondage of Egypt with enough silver and gold to finance their next season. We may not always understand what's going on in difficult moments. However, in time, as we see the beauty of God's sovereignty unfolding, pushing us toward our highest and greatest good, we will be able to accept that God is good and desires good things for us.

Prayer: *"Sovereign God, strengthen me today to walk by faith and not by sight. Even when I cannot see behind the scenes, I will rest in the knowledge that You have wonderful plans for me. Amen."*

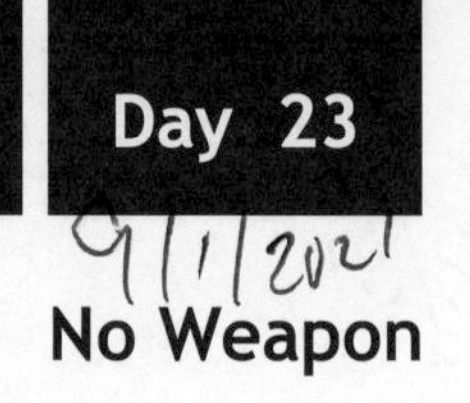

No Weapon

Affirmation

> *"What has not killed me has only made me stronger. The pressures in my life have only served to revealed my inner power. What my enemies meant for my demise, God has used for my good. Every failure and mistake are now important pieces of my wisdom. There are no weapons formed against me. There are only opportunities to grow and evolve."*

There is a scene in the movie *The Matrix* where a young child is effortlessly bending a spoon using only his mind. Neo, the main character and protagonist, asks the child how this is possible. The child responds, "Try to realize the truth…there is no spoon." In other words, I have power over this spoon because I know it doesn't exist. In spiritual terms, the material world is an illusion and at very least temporary or passing away. What if we could apply this same principle when dealing with perceived evil in our lives?

God enlightens Isaiah to this concept, *"See, it is I who created the blacksmith who fans the coals into flame, and forges a weapon fit for its work. And it is I who have created the destroyer to wreak havoc; no weapon forged against you will prevail"* (Isaiah 54:16-17). So, God created the creator of the weapon, the user of the weapon and indirectly the weapon itself. What does all of this mean? Maybe the truth is…there is no weapon. Perhaps what we have perceived as weapons in our lives were actually God ordained catalysts pushing us into our next season? The devil tested Jesus in the wilderness and Jesus came out of this testing stronger and prepared for His ministry. Paul had a *"thorn in his flesh"* that he called a *"messenger of Satan."* This thorn enabled Paul to remain humble enough to continue authoring the majority of the New Testament. What if the things we have been cursing are actually working together for our benefit?

> **Prayer:** *"God all by Yourself, I give thanks in everything knowing all life and existence flows from You. No weapon can prosper against me because there is no weapon. Amen."*

10/16/2021

9/2/2021

Honoring Our Ancestors

Affirmation

"Each day is a gift from God. As I honor each day, each moment, each breath I am consciously living in gratitude. The best way for me to honor those who have transitioned too early is for me to make the most of my time on earth. I will honor the people in my life who have passed away by gleaning wisdom from the lessons they taught me through their journey."

At some point during our earth journey, we will attend a funeral, memorial service or home-going celebration and grieve the loss of someone we knew and loved. Unfortunately, there are times we say goodbye to someone who we perceived passed away too soon or left unfinished business undone and purpose unrealized. We walk away feeling not only the grief of losing a loved one but also struggle with the regret that this person may have never fulfilled their life's destiny. There is an old saying "The graveyard is the wealthiest place on earth." In other words, many people with endless potential carry this wealth with them to the grave.

How do we honor their deaths? More importantly, how do we honor their lives? What if their lack of accomplishment, their mistakes and missteps, their incomplete journeys and the wealth they carried with them to the graveyard can actually serve a greater purpose? More than dedicating buildings to them or hanging their pictures in hallways, we can honor their lives and their deaths by soaking in the lessons they taught us. You may say "I don't remember them ever specifically teaching me any lesson." However, their successes and their failures are the unspoken lessons they leave to us as an inheritance and as an assignment. As we navigate our journeys using the wisdom of the lessons they left for us to utilize, we are bestowing upon them the highest of all honors.

Prayer: *"Giver of Life, enable me to honor all life by learning, and then living, the lessons left to me by my loved ones and ancestors. Today, I honor their passing by my living. Amen."*

9/3/2021 10/17/21

Room to Grow

Affirmation

"Just as a fish will only grow to the size of an aquarium, my mind will only expand to the size of its container. I will not allow the growth potential of my mind to be stunted by any limitation of race, religion, country, or culture. Today, I choose to live above label and free from any container. Today, I choose the mind of Christ!"

Have you ever been to a pet store and seen a large fish in a small aquarium? Sometimes the fish has lived its entire existence in that same small space. Other times, someone bought that fish and realized it's capacity and growth potential was more than they could handle and brought it back in desperation to the place they purchased it as a last resort. There is an old adage that a fish will only grow to the size of its container. In my 20's I got into tropical fish. One of the fish (called an Arowana) that I thought was especially beautiful was actually from the Amazon River. My Arowana grew to be almost two feet long. I was so proud of how big and beautiful he was. Until one day, I visited the Tennessee Aquarium and saw an Arowana in an aquarium about the size of my house. This Arowana was almost as big as me! I was both amazed and humbled. Obviously, I had limited my fish's growth potential by placing him into a container that didn't allow him to flourish and thrive. Yet, with my limited perspective I was living in pride.

Have you placed your mind into a container? Were you born into an environment that limited your potential? What are the boxes, boundaries, borders or barriers we place around our minds? Is it religion? Or only reading one religious book? Is it a boundary of color, culture or country? Make the choice today to never place your limitless, endless spirit into anything limiting. And, then give that same freedom to others.

Prayer: *"Spirit of Limitless Expansion, give me courage to live outside of religious systems or finite structures that would hinder my spiritual growth and awakening. My mind is open. I am ready to expand. Amen."*

Day 26

The WAY of Jesus

Affirmation

"I am aware that I cannot solve any problem by using the same consciousness that created it. Racial divides, religious wars and all segregations of the human family will only be solved as I create an environment of love and inclusion. Today, I will not only be a Christian…I will be a follower of THE WAY of Jesus. And, that WAY is LOVE!"

Jiddu Krishnamurti (philosopher and founder of the theosophical society) believed that a person practiced violence by labeling themselves as a Christian, Hindu, Muslim, etc. He believed that labeling encouraged separation, and separation eventually gave place to violence. Jesus left us several hints that He was more concerned with a person's thought process than their religion or label. He declared of the Centurion (a non-Jew and captain for the Roman oppression) that he had greater faith than anyone in Jerusalem. He told the disciples that He had *"sheep in other pastures"* that no one knew about. He told the woman at the well it didn't matter where she worshipped as long as she did it in Spirit. Jesus rebuked his disciples for condemning the Hellenists that didn't become His followers. He even scolded the Pharisees for making converts. Then He confuses the conversation by saying *"I am the Way the truth and the life. No one comes to God except through Me"* (John 14:6).

I wonder if Jesus meant no one comes to God unless they come through Him, His name and become a Christian? Or, unless they follow His Way… The Way of Jesus? The Way of love and higher thought. I believe promoting one religion over another is the cause of much of the strife in humanity. So, we cannot solve a problem (religious wars) using the same consciousness that created it (religious supremacy). Let us spend our time, money and energy, not converting people to Christianity, but convincing them of God's love…The Way of Jesus.

Prayer: *"Spirit of Unity, give me new a consciousness to create a world of peace and a beloved community of inclusion and coexistence. Amen."*

Day 27

10/19/21

9/5/2021

Let Me Be Spiritual

Affirmation

"Today I set my intention to make the main thing the main thing. I will not get lost in the smallness of rules, clothes, prayers or symbolism. I am an intelligent, awakened and self-aware spirit-being with the capacity and courage to see what is beneath the surface. I do not need a title, a reserved seat, a special parking space or a fancy robe to be spiritual. I AM created in the image and likeness of God and Good. And, tapping into my God-given Divinity is the most spiritual thing I will ever do!"

Rules. Regulations. Rituals. Restrictions. Regimens… Religion. Somewhere in the minutia of this mad monotony we lose sight of the main thing while desperately chasing a passing grade. Religion has a slow and subtle way of succeeding in attracting our attention to everything but the main thing. Jesus described this syndrome as *"straining at a gnat but swallowing a camel."* In other words, focusing on the things that really don't matter while forgetting and neglecting the things that do. Special diets, sacred days, sanctimonious robes, solemn symbols…all very important and unique to religious culture and expression. But, by no means the main thing.

Several years ago I spoke at a New Thought church for the first time. I was excited to have a new "spiritual" worship experience outside my religious norm. I was weary with religious literalism, predictable protocols and pretentious pageantry. At this New Thought Church, we were going to practice meditation. We were instructed how to hold our hands, breathe, etc. Yet, I did it a bit differently as my own way of connecting to God. I was told by a congregant I was doing it wrong. I politely explained I had enough religion and wanted to be spiritual. I believe she missed the point. Everyone worships, connects to Spirit their own way. Don't get lost in details or people's projections. Make the main thing the main thing. And, keep it that way.

Prayer: *"Common Sense, I desire to be spiritually free, not religiously restricted. Enable me to make the main thing love, peace and joy. Amen."*

Day 28

Protected by an Enemy

Affirmation

"I'm at peace with my PAST. The lessons, the hurt, the relationships I've lost and gained have all worked together for my good. I release the hurt. I bless and forgive those who did not know what they were doing. I do not need closure or an apology to move forward with seeking and pursuing peace in my life. I embrace the wisdom I gained from difficult lessons. I know that I will not learn those lessons again. And, I am aware that what threatened me in the past might protect me in the future."

When David fought against Goliath he had only a sling-shot and a few stones. After striking a deadly blow, David went over to the slain giant and cut off his head, using Goliath's own sword. Gruesome, I know. I'm going somewhere. Several years later, David rushes into a battle. In his haste, he fails to take any weaponry with him. When he arrives to the battleground he asks his men if there is anything he could use to fight. One of his captains tells him all of the weapons are already spoken for. However, the sword of Goliath (used mostly as a memorial and symbol of remembrance) was not being used. David grabbed Goliath's sword and went into the battle. Here is the lesson: The very thing that had threatened David's life in the past was now protecting him in the present, and potentially the future.

What threatened you in the past that is now presently protecting you? What former enemy is now a current friend? An accusation? Legal situation? Divorce? Bankruptcy? Pride? Ambition? Along life's journey all of us will experience a brush with devastation, even arrive at the brink of disaster. We'll be threatened by various predicaments and vengeful people. When we come through these anxious encounters we are blessed with a gift. We carry the gift of wisdom we gained with us forever. The very thing that threatened to kill us in our past is now anxious to protect us in our present and future. Let it!

Prayer: *"God of peace and calamity, I will give thanks in everything…for my past enemies now stand watch as my present protectors. Amen."*

Day 29

The Same...Yesterday, Today and Forever

Affirmation

"God is not changing…WE ARE! God is not changing…I AM! I am not my beliefs. I am not my opinions. I am the Spirit who is aware that I have beliefs and opinions. I am bigger than my thoughts. I am the Spirit capable of having thoughts and changing beliefs. I am open and available for Spirit to guide me to Higher Ground!"

As God's messenger, Moses proposed ideas like: wearing blended fabrics was an abomination, a young woman was worth twice as much as an older woman and an eye for an eye and a tooth for a tooth was God's way of justice. Interestingly, as we progress through the pages and books of the Bible, God seems to be growing, expanding in thought, awakening to new dimensions of higher consciousness and managing His anger in a more civilized manner. Jesus provides us with a peculiar predicament as He began many of His teachings by saying, *"you have heard of old, but I say to you."* In other words, Jesus was saying, whatever God said to Moses years ago…He has changed His mind over time. At one time, God wanted us to seek justice and exact revenge on anyone who harmed us. But now, God wants us to forgive and turn the other cheek. What amazing growth and maturity has taken place in God over the years! Is God changing? Or are we?

God, Creator of the heavens and the earth, the original vibration who formed the universe with His words and breathed life into man, is not changing…not getting better with time. The Bible is not a record of God's gradually advancing mindset or an account of God's diversifying cultural opinions. The Bible is a beautiful, sometimes brutal, story of man's journey toward awakening, enlightenment and expanded thought. God, who never changes, desires to carry us from wisdom to wisdom, glory to glory, one level to another, line upon line and precept upon precept. Let's agree to go.

Prayer: *"Changeless God, give me the courage to change and challenge my beliefs and opinions. I desire to go higher. Take me there. Amen."*

9/8/2021

The SPECK and the PLANK

Affirmation

"My life is too powerful and purposeful to waste it searching for the speck in my neighbor's eye. I will not make a habit of committing the spiritual sin of judging others. Instead, I will focus my mind on fully connecting with the unconditional love of God. Once I have been baptized in love, I will overcome my need to judge. God's love will enable me to see others through the eyes of love...only then will I be able to compassionately offer them help and restoration without judgment."

Jesus asks a very thought provoking question:

> *"why do we spend our time and energy searching for the speck in someone else's eye without considering the plank in our own eye?" (Matthew 7:1-5; Luke 6:41-42)*

A speck is a small thing. However, a plank is a much larger thing. In essence, Jesus is saying our desire to judge is the bigger issue here. The smaller issue is whatever another person may be struggling with in their own life. Unfortunately, many people focus more on another person's speck (their sin) than on their own plank (judgment of others).

We are encouraged to get rid of the plank (our desire to judge others) and then we will miraculously be able to see clearly and bring healing to others (help them remove the speck). Assisting others on their journey toward renewal and restoration can only be done with love and compassion.

> **Prayer:** *"Spirit of God, let me see through eyes of love today. Grant me the strength to build up, not break down. Give me the courage to restore, not condemn. Today, I surrender my need to judge others and open my heart and mind to be filled with Your love. I want to see others as You see them! Amen."*

Day 31

10/23/21

9/9/21

Creating God in My Image

Affirmation

"I will not create God in my own image by projecting my cultural biases, social prejudices and religious experiences onto God. I am willing to surrender to the truth that I am created in God's image, and not the other way around. I have studied to show myself approved. Now, I am ready and able to rightly divide between the word of man and the Logic of God! God is Spirit. And, today I choose to worship in Spirit and in Truth!"

We did not create God. God created us. More specifically, God created us in His image and likeness (Genesis 1:27). Strangely, so many religions, and religious people, get this backwards. They create God in their image. And, they're not alone. Moses, David, the Apostle Paul…many great men and inspired leaders and writers have committed the error of creating God in their image. Does God favor the firstborn son over the other sons? Does God allow us to own slaves as long as they are from a neighboring country and not our own? Does God discriminate against people who wear glasses? Does God sanction a man to speak in church but forbid a woman to speak? I think, or at least I truly hope, that all of us would laugh at these questions and answer "No!" Yet, these are all teachings we can find in the Bible…God's Word. These are all examples of man creating God in his image. The created, projecting its own ideas, cultural opinions and even prejudices, onto the Creator.

When we read the Bible, we must do so with both an open heart and a critical mind. The men who wrote the Bible, and the men who found denominations, have a tendency of projecting their own biases and beliefs onto others, and indirectly onto God, sadly, in the name of God. Ask God to help you rightly divide the Word of Truth. The Holy Spirit will grant you the ability to discern between man's temporary, changing opinions and God's eternal, unchanging truth.

Prayer: *"Creative Spirit, help me see when I create You in my image. Today, I surrender to being created in Your image and likeness. Amen."*

The Beginner's Mind

Affirmation

"Today I celebrate the BEGINNER'S MIND. I am the knowing and the unknowing. I am believing and disbelieving. I am learning and unlearning. In this present moment I surrender to the process of being transformed by the renewing of my mind."

Jesus introduced a concept to the religious order that didn't sit very well. He told them they *"must become like little children"* in order to enter the kingdom of God. They struggled to accept this teaching as they had worked tirelessly to be perceived as experts in their field. They had memorized laws, perfected rituals and become masters in their religion. Now Jesus has the audacity to suggest they voluntarily take a demotion, unlearn some of what they had spent years studying. And further, become open, curious and inquisitive? Like children? Unfortunately, they could not humble themselves to this place of openness. It seems they possessed zero capacity to celebrate the Beginner's Mind. Consequently, they were unable to believe, receive, or even perceive, the teachings of Jesus. Why? Because when you believe you have learned it all, there is no available space for new learning. In essence, you become a "know it all." There is also quite a bit of ego wrapped up in this resistance. Mastery brings with it benefits: better titles, reserved seating, higher salaries. Those who grow accustomed to the kickbacks of mastery are unwilling to take a demotion in the name of expanded consciousness. So, it was the uneducated, the unlearned, the untrained who received the message of Jesus. He even chose disciples who were young and inexperienced so He wouldn't have to wallow for years through the deep mud of religious indoctrination. Let's make the decision to leave some available space for God to continually bring us new and fresh revelation. Today, let's become like children. And, then stay that way.

Prayer: *"Daily Bread, I'm open and available for fresh manna and a living word. I'm not a 'know it all' and want to celebrate the Beginner's Mind. Give me the courage to become like a child. Amen."*

Day 33

9/11/2021 10/27/21

The Pee-Pee Prayer

Affirmation

"Today, I will think and thank from a higher vibration. I will think first, thank second and only ask as a last resort. I will count it all joy when I remember where God has brought me from. I will live, think, thank and speak from a place of power. As I give thanks IN all things, I am also declaring my healing FROM all things, and then navigating my way THROUGH all things!"

One of my mentors is famous for saying, "a thinking man is a thanking man." In other words, when we stop to think, we all have something to be thankful for. How do we live in a vibration of thanksgiving and approach life with an attitude of gratitude after we lose a job? Endure a painful divorce? When we have more bills than money? There are different levels of gratitude. At times, we must give thanks for life's journey, even when some of the pieces of our journey may be temporarily out of sync. I have noticed when I give thanks in one area of my life it becomes contagious and begins to affect other areas of my life. This is how vibration works. When you begin to raise your vibration in one area of your life it has a powerful effect on other areas of your life. So, get happy and see what happens! Or, don't wait 'til the battle's over…shout now!

I also like to give thanks for small things or things that might be easily taken for granted. Every morning I try to wake up in gratitude. When I wake up, I give thanks for being alive. I give thanks for being in my right mind. I give thanks for my lungs and for the breath in my body (especially after I brush my teeth). It may seem strange, but each morning when I use the restroom, I give thanks that my kidneys are working properly. Dr. Michael Beckwith talks about this in his book *Spiritual Liberation*. He refers to this as the "Pee-Pee Prayer." Sure it sounds silly. Yet, it is a good way to begin each day with thanksgiving rather than in stress, worry and anxiety.

Prayer: *"Fountain of Blessings, thank you for breath, life, health, strength and for a sound mind. Amen."*

Little Victories

10/26/2021

Affirmation

"Although change is constant and consistent throughout the universe, change can be a challenge in my life. As I embark on the journey of creating change and manifesting the life I want to experience, I am aware it will not happen all at once or overnight. I am looking for progress, not perfection. And, until I arrive at my destination, I will learn to celebrate the little victories along the way."

Before David faced Goliath, King Saul had a conversation with David trying to offer him advice as he faced this seemingly impossible mission. Surprising to Saul, David came across as very confident and prepared. Saul asked David why he felt he would experience victory against this giant. David let Saul know that this was not his first fight. David informed Saul that a lion had attacked his flock and that God gave him victory over the lion. Similarly, David shared a story about a bear attacking his flock and God had enabled him once again to overcome the bear. Finally, David lets Saul know that the same God who gave him power over a lion and a bear, would give him the victory over Goliath. David had learned to celebrate little victories along the way that gave him the courage and confidence to face a larger challenge in his life.

The prophet Elijah offers us a similar example. In Elijah's day, there was a severe drought. Elijah began to send out his servant to see if there was any rain on the horizon. Time after time, his servant came back with the report that there was no rain, and not even a cloud. Finally, on the seventh time, Elijah's servant comes back and tells him he saw a very small cloud about the size of a man's hand. Elijah celebrates this little victory and begins to declare that he hears *"the sound of abundant rain."* Celebrate little victories today. They have a way of becoming bigger victories!

Prayer: *"Victorious God, today I give thanks for little victories and I trust You are able to turn little victories into big victories. You have delivered me in the past. I know You can do it again! Amen."*

Day 35

Creating Good

Affirmation

"I am created in the image and likeness of God. That means I am creative like God. I have the power to create good. And, I have the power to create evil. I am learning to use this power the way God intended. I am a mature spiritual creature. This means, I don't need the threat of hell in order to do what is good and right. I do good because I came from Divine Good, and because I am good! I love God without the promise of heaven or the threat of hell. I love God because God is God!"

Creative power is neutral. It is neither good nor bad. Similar to all forms of power, creative power is completely at the mercy of the mind wielding it. The good or evil produced totally depends on the way it is used. This creative power is sometimes referred to as "free will" in religious and theological circles. This is exactly what it is…freedom to use our divine creative power any way we want. This wonderful freedom is potentially very dangerous. To be plain, our freedom can enslave us. We are free to create peace and prosperity. Conversely, we are also free to create sorrow and suffering. The freedom isn't to be blamed. The Creator who endowed us with this freedom isn't to be blamed. Learning to navigate this freedom, for good purposes, is the reason we incarnate and come to earth. In essence, we are learning, on a smaller scale, how to handle being like God. How do we control this power?

One of the ways religion has attempted to control this creative power is by incentives, or the promise of rewards (and the fear of consequences). If you create good, you go to heaven. If you create evil, you go to hell. On the surface, this doesn't seem so harmful, until a majority of people begin doing good to get to heaven instead of doing good for the sake of doing good. Ulterior motives, lower vibrations and base levels of consciousness are the results of these fear driven strategies and we wind up serving God out of fear or some hidden manipulation. Let's do good…because we are good!

Prayer: *"God of Freedom. Today, I know there is an open door set before me. I can choose life or death. I choose life! Amen."*

10/28/2021

The IS-ness of God's Love

Affirmation

"I cannot earn or un-earn God's love. God's love is not a response or reaction to anything. God IS love. Nothing can separate me from God's love. Nothing can separate God from being God. And, nothing can keep God from being love. Today, I understand a mystery...that I have boldness in the day of judgment. Because as He is...so am I! Perfect love casts out fear. And today, I will allow my love to conquer any fear."

1 John 4:8 tells us that *"God is love."* The key word here is *"IS."* Notice, the word here is *"IS,"* not *"DOES."* God doesn't love...God IS love. This means God's love for us flows out of His essence and nature. Love is the essence of God. We may perceive it as the action of God, but it does not come from God as an action. It emits from God as essence. So, God's love to us, and to all, is not an action, reaction or response to anything. This means, we cannot earn or un-earn God's love. God does not give or take away His love from us. The reason we cannot be separated from God's love is because God cannot be separated from God or detoured from being God. God's love is perfect because it cannot be recalled or retracted. And, our understanding of God's perfect love nature is what casts out our fear!

"In this is love, not that we loved God, but that He loved us" (1 John 4:10). We love God because God first loved us. Our love is a response. But, God's love to us is not a response. Our challenge is to learn to love like God... not as a response to love, but because love IS who we are! Jesus challenged the disciples to this level of love by instructing them to love their enemies, not just their family and friends who loved them. In other words, Jesus was saying, don't love as a response to being loved. Let love be your essence. This way, no person and no situation could ever change who you are. In every circumstance, you are always being you. Always being love! Just like God!

Prayer: *"Perfect Love, give me the strength to become love. Today, I desire not only to love others. I want to be love. Amen."*

 October 29, 2021

Free FROM Sin and Free TO Sin

Affirmation

"In the Christ Reality, I am free from sin, even if my mind does not perceive it yet. I cannot offend God. I can only miss the mark of my own divinity. In other words, I can only sin against myself. Today, I am free FROM sin. And, I am free TO sin. However, that doesn't mean I will create hell for myself. I will ask for wisdom from God concerning how to utilize my divine creativity to create the abundant life I want to experience."

While baptizing one day, John suddenly looked up and saw his cousin Jesus. Describing Jesus, John said, *"Behold the Lamb of God who takes away the sin of the world"* (John 1:29). The word sin in this verse is actually the Greek word *hamartia* which means "to offend God." Jesus, the Lamb of God, has taken away the world's ability to offend God. Wow! So, if we no longer offend God, how do we sin? In the first epistle of John we find out that we do sin, but in a different way and against a different entity. *"My little children, these things I write to you, so that you may not sin. And if anyone sins, we have an Advocate"* (1 John 2:1). The use of sin here is the Greek word *hamartano* which means "to miss the mark." So, when we sin now, it no longer offends God. However, it is a missing of the mark? What mark? And, who's mark? And, who are we sinning against if God is not offended? We are sinning against ourselves. And, we are missing the mark of our own divinity by falling beneath our own godlikeness.

The Apostle Paul received a revelation of this when he declared *"all things were lawful"* for him, but all things were not helpful and did not edify (1 Corinthians 6:12; 10:23). Paul also declared that although he was free to do all things, he did not want be to *"brought under the control"* of anything. So, we are free from sin and free to sin, and still be loved by God. Yet, we are encouraged to not miss the mark by creating hell for ourselves or for others.

Prayer: *"Lamb of God, thank you for taking away the offense. Today, empower me not to miss the mark. Amen."*

Old Dogs and New Tricks

Affirmation

"I am open and available for the Universe to send me whatever is necessary for the evolution of my soul. I boldly declare I am free from the lower mind and from literal thinking. I am not my beliefs and I am surrendered to the process of Spirit taking me from glory to glory."

There is an old saying, "An old dog can't learn a new trick." Fortunately, you're not a dog, even if you consider yourself to be old. We are here to grow, evolve, unfold and surrender to being *"transformed into the image"* of God (2 Corinthians 3:18). So, along our transformational journey we will encounter situations, sometimes challenging ones, all designed to develop us into our higher selves. The disciple Peter is a prime example of this.

Peter is in desperate need of growth. Peter is a racist and a misogynist. Peter believes that only his Jewish brethren are worthy of being accepted into the family of God. So, God (the Universe) sends Peter what is necessary for the evolution of his consciousness. God gives Peter a vision of unclean animals and tells Peter to eat them. But, the vision is really a metaphor for Peter to understand that God is asking him to accept the Gentiles (or people from other countries and cultures) into the fold. When Peter awakens from the vision, God sends him to the house of Cornelius (a well-known Gentile). When Peter arrives at Cornelius' house he encounters Gentiles (people from other countries he doesn't accept or include) experiencing the presence of God. Peter finally gets the point of God provoking, poking, pushing and prodding him. Peter has the revelation that *"God is no respecter of persons."* God wouldn't leave Peter alone until he grew and evolved. And, there is good news for us all. God won't leave us alone until we surrender to this process of transformation.

Prayer: *"Divine Change Agent, I surrender to the process of being transformed into my highest expression of divinity. Today, I ask You to send to me whatever is necessary for my unfoldment. Amen."*

Day 39

October Sunday 31, 2021

The Middle Way

Affirmation

"I am balanced, stable, moderate and at peace walking the Middle Way. I am not attracted to extremes or gimmicks. Today, I confess that I am clothed in my right mind and seated at the feet of Jesus."

The Middle Way is a Buddhist teaching that encourages balance by avoiding extremes. The Middle Way suggests that we not be overly given to self-indulgence or self-denial; over-eating or starvation; sexual promiscuity or asceticism; hilarity or seriousness. The Middle Way could be described as practicing the wisdom of moderation. I have observed human behavior, as it relates to religious practice, for most of my life. Many I have observed get extremely excited about their relationship with God and attend every church service possible, set early morning prayer times, go on all manner of fanatical fasts depriving themselves of food and any form of fun. These types never successfully find the Middle Way. And, as a result, their extreme lifestyle leads to exhaustion, sensory overload and eventually a strong sense of guilt and self-criticism over their inability to maintain their imbalanced commitments.

On one occasion, one of these fanatical types called me at 3:00 a.m. to discuss a particular Bible verse. I told him my wife and children were asleep and that we could talk in the morning at an appropriate hour. He ridiculed me for my lack of hunger for God. Less than one month later he was done with his unsustainable exuberance and done with church altogether. Twenty-eight years later, I am still walking the Middle Way and growing in Spirit at a steady, consistent and balanced pace. The Apostle Paul asks a question *"you ran well, but what did hinder you?"* Or, you started strong, but then you burned out…or perhaps lost balance? Whether it is exercise, work, spending, volunteer work…there exists a balanced path that allows for stability, consistency and longevity. Find it!

Prayer: *"Sustainer God, teach me the ways of balance. Give me the passion and pace, the wisdom and way, to endure to the end. Amen."*

Overcoming the Ego

Affirmation

"I am not what I have, do, or what others think of me. I am not separate from others or from God. And, I am not separate from what's missing in my life! I am the artist painting and sculpting the masterpiece of my life. My thoughts are like seeds. And today, I choose to grow flowers…not weeds!"

Immediately after His baptism, Jesus spent 40 days in the wilderness being tempted by the Devil. After a closer look, we find that Jesus was actually *"driven by the Spirit to the wilderness to be tempted by the Devil"* (Matthew 4:1). Why would the Spirit drive Jesus to the Devil? When we research the nature of these temptations, we can clearly see Jesus is being forced to deal with His ego and face His lower human nature. During this testing, Jesus would face issues like identity, desire for fame and possessions. This process of Jesus overcoming His ego corresponds with how Dr. Wayne Dyer described the ego. Dr. Dyer defined the ego this way: *"I am what I have. I am what I do. I am what others think of me."* So, overcoming the ego is a process of retraining how we see ourselves. It might be helpful to turn it around: I am not what I have. I am not what I do. And, I am not what others think of me.

When we are able to see ourselves minus the dependency on our possessions, without the blinding glare of our career or calling and separate from the inordinate attachment to other people's opinions of us, we find it easier to clear our minds of expectations and judgments. Then, we find new ways of defining success. We experience victory over criticism. And, we discover an immunity to flattery. With this new clarity, we are able to create life without the constant interference of the ego. In essence, we can plant new seeds without the threat of old weeds. When the weeds of ego are gone all that remains is Spirit. You are bigger than anyone's definition of you…even your own.

Prayer: *"God above definition, enable me to create my life from a clear mind, without judgment, void of criticism and free of ego. Amen."*

Day 41 November 2, 2021

Grace Abuse

Affirmation

"Today, I am grateful for the grace of God in my life. And, I am deeply thankful for the price Jesus paid to offer me this free gift. However, I will not be guilty of grace abuse, or allow any idea of an unlimited supply of grace to lure me into an ongoing destructive pattern. I will not use grace as a crutch keeping me from becoming more like Christ or hindering me from learning to use my divine creativity to create the life I want to experience."

I grew up under the teaching that our good works are like *"filthy rags"* and that salvation was *"not of works, lest anyone should boast."* I was taught that salvation was a "Finished Work" and I couldn't add anything to it. I don't believe this was intentionally meant to be harmful. It was just a way of promoting the strength of the cross or the power of the blood of Jesus. Although, it did become a bit of a bragging point and was common practice across the Evangelical world to actually diminish other religions (that taught personal growth) because they had to actually work on their character and become better people in order to reach Nirvana, or become enlightened, or find whatever their expression of heaven or eternal life might be.

There are some unintended problems with this expression of grace. Mainly, it requires no growth. All one must do is believe and confess Jesus as Savior. The result is people leaning solely on grace and never dealing with the condition of their heart. So, we have "followers" of Christ not following Christ. Hate, racism, homophobia, misogyny and discrimination of all sorts are tolerated, and sadly, promoted. As Christians, shouldn't we be on a path to becoming like Christ? There is also a strain of grace abuse dangerously allowing and promoting that people can do whatever they want because they can't lose the grace of God. Which is true. However, the devastation reaped with undisciplined living is a pain no one wants and a collateral damage no friend or loved one deserves.

Prayer: *"God of Grace, I desire to be more than a Christian. I want to be more like Jesus. Give me the grace to get there. Amen."*

I Deserve Good

11/3/21

Affirmation

"Today I am finally aware, and fully awake to the truth, that I create my life experience by my thoughts, words and choices. However, I am also aware that I don't deserve some of the things I have created. I can even completely own the negative things I create without being convinced that I deserve anything negative in my life. Because I am created from love and by a loving Creator, I know that I deserve love, peace, joy and happiness! Anything and anyone who tells me differently must be silenced!"

Many people, even entire families, have a long history of reaping difficult consequences associated with poor choices and negative thinking. When this vicious cycle repeats, often times people begin to believe there is no existence other than what they are experiencing. Even worse, people accept a false reality that somehow they don't deserve anything better. The pain and disappointment they have grown accustomed to just becomes their "plight" in life. And the most dysfunctional, destructive mindset is convinced that somehow this perpetual suffering is God's will and ultimately unalterable.

Bad things happen to good people…to all people. Sometimes it is entirely coincidence. Other times people think, speak, believe and then manifest bad things unknowingly and subconsciously via ignorance to their divine creative capacity. Whatever the case, we all deserve good things. If you create peace by consciously creating it, you deserve peace. If you plant seeds of drama and pain, you will reap the harvest of your creation. This doesn't mean you deserve it. Sowing and reaping, action and reaction, give and take, what goes around comes around, karma, are universal laws operating as exact sciences. We reap what we sow! Nonetheless, your Creator desires for you to be at peace and live in prosperity. Don't convince yourself you don't deserve good things. You do! Start creating good today!

Prayer: *"Ultimate Good, I know the plans You have for me and that You desire good things for me. Help me to accept that I deserve them. Amen."*

Is It Working For You?

11/4/2021

Affirmation

"Today, I am aware that there are many ways to find peace. Everyone's path is different and no two journeys are exactly the same. I will not spend my life arguing with others about their chosen path. Instead, I will ask myself the only question that really matters: Is It Working For Me?"

Some people find peace through religious literalism (adhering to a strict code of behaviors and rituals). Some find peace through meditation. Yet, others find peace by serving others. Whether a person finds peace through deep study or physical exercise, always be aware it is their path, and their peace. The personal path to peace is not a "one size fits all." Projecting your path onto others is a sure way to keep peace at a distance and encourage people to practice social distancing with you. Some people need closure. Others need a new landscape. Assuming that everyone must walk the same path or connect to Source using the same method, in the end, only threatens your own peace as you will struggle with the frustration of wondering why they don't realize how right you are. The reality is…the only universal truth that applies to universal truth is allowing each person their own universal truth. Learn to respect other people's journeys and you will inevitably find peace for yourself.

Arguing over who is right, who's perspective is the most accurate, who's path is the straightest, will ultimately only serve to create a chasm between family and friends. The only question we should concern ourselves with is: IS IT WORKING FOR ME? And, what works for me may not work for all those I love. Arguments over right and wrong will never be satisfied. Furthermore, knowing what works for me in this season may not work forever or even in my next season. Allow people their own path to God. And, encourage them to change at their own pace and in their own space.

Prayer: *"Universal God, I am aware there are many ways to connect to You. Today, I will allow everyone to find their own connection. Amen."*

Guilty Peace

11/5/2021

Affirmation

"The Kingdom of God is righteousness, peace and joy in the Spirit. And, the Kingdom of God is within. Today, from my inner man, I choose peace. I also choose to be at peace without feeling any guilt. Others who are not experiencing peace will attempt to make me feel guilty for my peace. But, if I enter their vibration I will not be able to infect them with my peace. I am at peace with my journey, I am at peace with my God, I am at peace with myself and I am at peace with being at peace."

The *"peace of God," "the Prince of Peace", a "peace that surpasses understanding," "My peace I give you," "peace be still"*...these are all ways, names or biblical phrases describing peace. So, why is peace so rare in religious circles? Why do we sense a feeling of guilt being subtly placed on us by religious people when we find peace? There are justifications for lacking peace: someone else stole it; I had nothing to do with creating this drama. There are even spiritual ways of describing the lack of peace: I am so important to the Kingdom of God the devil is always fighting me; God is trusting me with a test right now...like Job. Whatever way we find to explain it, we are still making the strong admission that we don't have peace.

The Apostle Paul defines the Kingdom of God as *"righteousness, peace and joy in the Holy Spirit."* These three fruits of the Spirit seem to be missing from the produce sections of most churches. Most churchgoers struggle to accept that they are righteous, peace is hiding somewhere under the pews, and joy is just not appropriate because seriousness is so much more religious. Even worse, when a person truly learns how to create peace and maintain it, those who insist on creating fear, living in jealousy and guarding their turf, project guilt onto the peaceful few. Find peace by creating it. And, don't let anyone make you feel guilty about it!

Prayer: *"Abiding Peace, give me the wisdom to create peace, the courage to keep it and the nerve to resist those trying to guilt me for it! Amen."*

Get Back Up...Again

11/6/202

Affirmation

"Today, the Resurrection is alive and well as it is happening in me! The love, the light and the life of Jesus are waking up on the inside of me. As I show kindness, as I express care, as I extend help to the hurting, as I spread hope, the Resurrection is happening through me. Jesus is alive today. And, the Spirit of Jesus is alive within me."

Easter is a big day for churches. And, Easter is a lot of pressure for most pastors. There is an unspoken expectation from the faithful members that one sermon, specifically the Easter sermon, is going to transform all of the first timers and members, who only attend once a year on Easter, into somehow miraculously becoming weekly attenders. And, by the way, this magical sermon is to be short enough not to interfere with families pre-planned events. After about 20 years of killing myself to deliver a "best of the best" sermon every Easter, I realized that Easter, for people who don't have a weekly spiritual practice, is really just a social event, a pseudo high school reunion or a fashion show. So, what is Easter?

Easter is the powerful hope that as Jesus rose from the grave, so can we. But, in most Christian circles we believe our resurrection is a future event, when Christ calls all of the sleeping faithful saints out of their graves to meet Him in the sky. Easter is not only a future event. Easter is now, today, when we wake up to it. Because He lives, I can face tomorrow...not next year. The same Spirit that raised Christ from the dead is in us, the Kingdom is within us, Christ in us is the hope of glory. This means we can get back up now...from poor choices, financial ruin, divorce, sickness or from the heavy burden of guilt. We all fall down. But, we get up. And, because *"a righteous man may fall seven times,"* we may be getting back up...again. Easter is about resurrection, redemption and restoration. Today!

Prayer: *"Resurrection Power, awaken the power of Easter within me today. By Your Spirit, I will get back up...and get back up again. Amen."*

The Blame Game

Affirmation

"Blame is the subtle way I give my power away. Shame is the way I forbid my power from returning. I will not play the blame game or allow shame to keep me from re-creating my life. I will own, harness and learn to navigate the use of my divine creative capacity without any connection to blame or shame."

In the Garden of Eden metaphor, Adam and Eve are only forbidden one thing…not to eat of *"the tree of the knowledge of good and evil."* After they make the decision to eat or learn of this knowledge, they realize they are naked and attempt to cover and hide themselves. God descends to them in the garden and asks Adam why he has done this. Adam responds by saying *"It was the woman You gave me."* In Adam's response, we find two separate blames. Adam blames the woman, Eve. And, Adam indirectly blames God for giving him this woman. God then asks Eve why she has done this. Eve responds, *"it was the serpent."* So, Eve has blamed the serpent (or the devil) for making her do this. Adam nor Eve take any responsibility for their choice. In this case, shame leads to blame. And ultimately, shame and blame lead Adam and Eve away from God's Presence and keep them from waking up to their divine creative power.

This process exists all around us. One political party blames the other. One race blames all others. Churchgoers blame the devil (and occasionally God). Spouses blame spouses. Parents blame children. Children blame parents (even adult children blame parents). Sometimes people other than us are actually guilty and blameful. However, mostly we are directly involved with the realities we experience. In either case, when someone or something outside of us is always to be blamed, we are admitting that we have no power and continue to unconsciously give our power away. Reclaim your power today by refusing to give it away via shame and blame.

Prayer: *"Giver of Power, thank you for giving me power. Help me reclaim my divine power by not giving it away to anything outside of myself. Amen."*

Day 47

The Knowledge of Good and Evil

Affirmation

"Today I will not eat of the tree of the knowledge of good and evil. Instead, I will know that all things are from God, of God, through God, work for God, consist in God and will return to God. It's all good and all God."

Let's stay right here in the Garden of Eden metaphor. Whether there was an actual garden and a tree of knowledge with literal fruit really should not be our focus. I have witnessed, more than once, people debating whether the fruit Adam and Eve ate was an apple or a pomegranate. The truth is missed when we give our attention to arguing over where the garden was located and if there was actually a talking snake. The truth is in what all of these things represent. The garden is a place of innocence, peace and goodness. The tree of knowledge is the only thing threatening this divinely ordained existence. In this garden, all of the trees were good to eat from. The only forbidden tree was the one that made a judgment about the other trees or truths. Trees represent truths.

So, we could say all of the truths in the garden were good. The tree of knowledge represents the potential for religious division, disunity, dissension, discord and eventually destruction. We can apply this symbolism to every piece of our individual lives as well as the way we experience the world around us. Things happen to us (or through us) every day. They all have purpose (good) and can be significant in waking us up to our divine potential. Judging the experiences of our lives as bad causes a division of our minds, or double-mindedness. Furthermore, judging one tree (or truth, religion, philosophy, etc.) as evil only causes separation, breeds violence and forces us to leave the garden of peace. Unity with ourselves, harmony between religions and being at peace with God all begins with one choice...don't eat of the tree of the knowledge of good and evil.

Prayer: *"Eternal Good, open my eyes to see that all things are working together for my good. Amen."*

11/9/2021

Count It All Joy

Affirmation

"Today, I will count it all joy having confidence that faith-testing trials will teach me patience, and patience will bring a completeness and perfection in my life. I am grateful for the wisdom I have gleaned and remain open to receive more. I am persuaded that God wants to share wisdom with me. I live in gratitude for a benevolent universe that responds to my openness and sends the Teacher when I, the student, am ready for Him to appear!"

Count it joy when we face hardships? Joy in tests? Joy in trials? We may find it difficult to feel joy (or even want to) while we are in the middle of stressful seasons. Look closely at the order of how James describes goodness unfolding throughout challenging times:

"My brethren, count it all joy when you fall into various trials, knowing that the testing of your faith produces patience. But let patience have its perfect work, that you may be perfect and complete, lacking nothing. If any of you lacks wisdom, let him ask of God, who gives to all liberally and without reproach, and it will be given to him" (James 1:2-5).

Trials bring Testing…the Testing develops Patience… Patience yields Completeness/Perfection…the end result is that there is no lack of anything. And, as an added bonus, if we still don't have wisdom after this process is over, we can simply ask God and it will be given to us. The Bible describes Jesus approaching His most difficult moment (the cross) with a *"joy set before Him."* If we could see the end result of these growth pangs, we would be able to set a joy before us. Or, as we said in church growing up, not "wait 'til the battle is over…Shout Now!" It's all good and all God. And, we can count it all joy knowing it's not happening to us…it's happening for us!

Prayer: *"God of Joy, today I give thanks for the process of You developing me into my highest and greatest good. Amen."*

Clearing Out Space

11/10/2021

Affirmation

> *"Today, I am ready to clear out space and provide God room to create new life. I will not force new wine into old wineskins. I readily invite the Holy Spirit to guide me into all truth, new truth and higher truth."*

Genesis 1:1 *"In the beginning, God created..."* The 5th word in the Bible is *"created." Created* in Hebrew is *bara* – meaning to carve away, reshape and clear out space. So, this text (originally written in Hebrew) should read, *"In the beginning, God carved away, reshaped and cleared out space."* If God was clearing out space, reshaping, this means there was something to reshape...something in the way needing to be cleared out. You can't reshape, carve away or clear out something that is not there. With this knowledge, we can now say this text should read, *"In a beginning, God carved away, reshaped and cleared out space."* Now it should make more sense to us when the very next verse says, *"the earth was without form and void."* In a beginning, or the Genesis account of this specific beginning, God was reshaping and clearing out space, not just to create, but to re-create or create again! And, in order for God to bring order to chaos, light to darkness and design to void, there had to be a clearing out of the old to create the new.

When we experience God's love and begin the journey of awakening to the Christ Mind, the Genesis process of creation, re-creation and reshaping begins within us. We must be willing to clear out old thoughts, reshape our hearts and carve away the old mind to make room for the new man. Unfortunately, most Christians are like concrete...all mixed up and permanently set. We desire a new start and for God to re-create in us a clean heart and renew a right spirit within us. The challenge is that we must be willing to clear out space (or release old thoughts) for God to re-create a new life, a new mind, a new consciousness within us.

> ***Prayer:*** *"Re-Creating Spirit, reshape, clear out and carve away anything that keeps me from my highest and greatest good. Amen."*

11/11/2021

The Peace of God and Your Piece of God

Affirmation

"The Peace of God is bigger than my piece of God as the Peace of God surpasses all understanding and surpasses my specific understanding. I will not allow my piece of God to keep the Peace of God from becoming a reality among the global human family. I will let there be peace on earth. I will let it begin with me. And, I will consciously create peace by not allowing my piece to prevent peace!"

The ego is to be blamed for so much of the separation, disunity and violence that has existed between different religions, and human beings, for as long as there has been recordable human history. One religion's piece of God perpetually gets in the way of the Peace of God. From the three Hebrew children being forced to worship King Nebuchadnezzar's god, to Jewish Pharisees sending Jesus to the cross over religious differences, to the Christian's crusading and forcing Muslims to convert to Christianity, our history as a species is replete with one religion's piece of God preventing peace between all of God's children.

Somehow the Universe keeps presenting us with the opportunity to learn this same lesson (the lesson of tolerance and co-existence) over and over. Yet, we keep refusing the learning. Time and again, millennia after millennia, war after war, we continue to resist the lesson and insist that our specific piece of God is really the answer to finally experiencing the Peace of God. Once everyone believes exactly like us, uses our name for God, reads our specific Holy Book, worships like us, there will be peace on earth? Hold your piece of God close to your heart. And, never forget the spiritual tradition that introduced you to the Creator of the Universe. Yet, allow all of God's children the same right. Perhaps when all the pieces of God can agree to this Golden Rule, we will finally have the Peace of God.

Prayer: *"God of All, as Your child, I give thanks for my piece of You. Today, my piece won't prevent peace between all of Your children. Amen."*

Sound Doctrine

11/12/2021

Affirmation

"Sound Doctrine is not tainted by culture, subject to gender, influenced by race, partial to any era of history or area of the world. Sound Doctrine is not hostage to opinion, conscious of geography, biased to politics and never speaks from prejudice. Sound Doctrine does not choose sides, have favorites or show partiality. Sound Doctrine is timeless, universal and exists above humanity's attempt to create God in its own image."

One of my mentors passed along a piece of wisdom to me over 20 years ago that still resonates with me. He said, "Any doctrine that is worth keeping will accomplish three things: 1. Bring glory to God, 2. Create peace on earth, and 3. Foster goodwill between men." When Jesus was born, an angel laid the foundation for Sound Doctrine by announcing, *"Glory to God in the highest, And on earth peace, goodwill toward men."* (Luke 2:14).

Does the doctrine of hell and eternal torture bring glory to God? Does the promotion of one religion as supreme above all others create peace on earth? Does favoring one sect of God's children over another foster goodwill between men? I would hope the answer to all three of these questions would be "No!" So, Sound Doctrine must be accepted as being sound on more of a foundation than because some man from a specific culture and geographical area of the world claims God told him his race was chosen, that God favored the firstborn son over the others and that God permitted slavery as long as you didn't enslave your own race of people. Arriving at Sound Doctrine requires common sense, critical thinking and an ability to find objectivity above the temptations of cultural and tribal influences. Sound Doctrine begins with one idea: God is love.

Prayer: *"Timeless Truth, equip me to bring You glory, empower me to create peace on earth and enable me to foster goodwill between men. Amen."*

Flying Above the Turbulence

Affirmation

"Today, I will fly above the turbulence of lower thought. I will raise my vibration and watch as my thought life elevates me above the storms of small thinking and the strain of small-minded people. I consciously choose to create something new and different today!"

I have flown hundreds of times. Occasionally, I have flown through storms, some a little scarier than others. I remember the first time I flew, or rode nervously, through a storm. I looked out of the window nearest me and I could visibly see an immense storm ahead. Immediately, the plane began to shake and drop and I watched as the flight attendants found their seats very quickly. Suddenly, the pilot changed the trajectory and raised our altitude. The plane rose above the dark clouds, and amazingly, I could see the sun again. The shaking stopped, the plane stabilized and everyone on board breathed a sigh of relief as the flight attendants calmly brought them their peanuts and ginger ale.

There is always peace to be found. However, if we encounter, inherit or even create a storm, continuing to fly in the same way will not render us peace. The turbulence caused by gossip, worry, fear or any lower level of consciousness, cannot be overcome by continuing to create it. There must be a conscious decision to rise above and seek out a new altitude and attitude. When we fall into a pit, or even dig one ourselves, the absolute first choice to be made, if we want to get out of the pit, is to stop digging. Once we recognize the behavior and thought life that created turbulence, we can then rise above it and find the peace that has seemed so elusive. There is peace above the storm and even peace in the very eye of the storm. It can all be found by raising the level of our vibration and tapping into higher thoughts like love, trust, forgiveness, openness, flexibility and calmness.

Prayer: *"Calmer of the storm, give me the strength to rise above the turbulence created by lower thinking. Amen."*

Day 53

11/14/2021

Why Is This Happening...Again?

Affirmation

"Today, I will see what I have created, not be surprised by it and consciously create the life experience I desire. Nothing is happening to me. All of life is happening through me. I am awake to my divine capacity to create. And today, I will create consciously."

There are three different levels of awareness from which we create life. We create our lives consciously, subconsciously and unconsciously. How do we know which level of creative awareness we are operating from? To be honest, most people create life from the middle, or from a mixture, of all three levels of awareness (even those who are self-aware and self-actualized). When things show up in our lives that completely shock us and catch us off guard, we are likely creating unconsciously. If we continually ask the question, "why is this happening to me?" we are probably creating life unconsciously. If we ask the question, "why is this happening to me AGAIN?" we are definitely creating life unconsciously. Most of the time we create life subconsciously or from the middle ground of our conscious awareness. Subconscious creativity is a bit like driving on cruise control. We are aware. We are involved. But, we are also allowing the machines, mechanisms and daily environments to drive. In subconscious creativity, when events or situations arise we are not shocked and we actually have some level of remembrance with our choices and thought life that invited this experience into our reality. When we create consciously we are not caught off guard by our life reality. Rather, we are fully awake to what we think, completely connected to what we choose, and when our outer world begins to reflect our inner thoughts we are not surprised because we have already received the RSVP that these things were going to show up. We are more powerful than we have ever imagined. When we create consciously we are harnessing our God-given ability and right to operate in divine creativity.

Prayer: *"Conscious Creator, awaken me today to create my life from a conscious mind. I desire to be fully awake. Amen."*

11/15/2021

Inclusion Conversion

Affirmation

"As I ascend to new levels of consciousness and spirituality I will celebrate where I am, where I have been and where I am going. However, I will not project my individual journey onto others. Everyone changes. But, they change at their own pace and in their own space. I will trust that the same Spirit working in me is also working in others and in all of creation. I will surrender to the idea that spirituality is not a 'one size fits all.' I will remember that what works for me may not work for everyone. If the opportunity presents itself, I will gladly and respectfully share the beauty of my awakening without forcing it on anyone."

I was raised in an Evangelical Christian environment. This means many things. But, for the sake of today's affirmation, it meant we were commissioned to convert other people, actually all people everywhere, to think and believe like us. People from other religions, and atheists of no religion, were the potential "harvest." And, our job was to get out there into the "highways and hedges," into "the systems of the world," into the "field," and reap the harvest by successfully converting them to our religion…even to the specific denominational and doctrinal expression of our religion.

As I journeyed through my religious experience, I began to undergo a steady, and occasionally quantum, transformation. My theology evolved. My understanding of the nature and character of God changed. I became much more inclusive in my approach and much more expansive in my thought and theology. Everything about my understanding of God and the universe shifted. However, I unconsciously drug my Evangelical practice of conversion into my new way of seeing God. I no longer sought to get anyone saved. But, I did pressure people to see and accept my new understanding as their own. I was attempting to convert the world to inclusion. I recognized it, shifted and gave it to God.

Prayer: *"Inclusive Love, thank You for shifting me, shaping me and sharing with me. I trust You are doing this with all of Your children. Amen."*

11/16/2021

To Me. Around Me. Through Me. As Me. For Me.

Affirmation

"Today, I will be aware that life is not happening to me or around me. I am awake to the truth that life is happening through me, as me and ultimately for me. I am not a helpless victim without options or power. I am not an innocent bystander watching as life is created around me. I am a change agent and conscious participant in the creation of my life."

The *"same Spirit that raised Christ from the dead"* is living in us. We are positioned to do greater things or *"greater works"* than Christ. We are *"more than conquerors."* We *"can do all things through Christ." "Christ in us is the hope of glory."* We are *"made in the image and likeness of God"* and can *"behold in the mirror the glory of God."* Wow! So, we are not wretches saved by grace, lowly worms born in sin and shaped in iniquity or Adam's fallen helpless race. We are *"the righteousness of God in Christ," "predestined for good works"* and ordained before we showed up in our mother's wombs.

What does all of this good news mean? It means we are more powerful than we ever imagined. Life is not happening TO US (victim mentality). Life is not happening AROUND US (bystander mentality). Life is happening THROUGH US (participant mentality). Life is happening AS US (divinely awake mentality). And, life is happening FOR US (goodness of God mentality). These are five different lenses that we use to perceive life. Two of these lenses are power-thieves (To me, Around me). Seeing life as happening to us or around us places us in a never-ending cycle of blameful bitterness and eventually becomes an endless existence of powerlessness, poverty and paralysis. Conversely, three of these lenses are power-boosters (Through me, As me, For me). Our thoughts, words and choices show up as our lives. When we see life this way, we reclaim our creative power and realize that it is all working through us, as us and for us.

Prayer: *"God of Power, strengthen me to create my life consciously from a position of power and purpose. Amen."*

11/17/21

All Things To All People

Affirmation

"Regardless of race, gender, culture, religion, language, sexual orientation, economic status, politics, geography or country of origin, I have something in common with every other human being on this planet that I come in contact with. I am open to seeing our commonalities and I will endeavor to find ways of connecting with all of the global human family."

The Apostle Paul famously wrote *"I become all things to all people..."* (1 Corinthians 9:22). This verse has been much maligned by many fear-based Christians with comments like: "If you're all things to everyone you're nothing to no one," and "If you don't stand for something you'll for anything." Finding common ground with people doesn't mean you immediately become brainwashed by them or give up all that is sacred to you. When you are confident in who you are, you have no need to approach every new connection with fear and suspicion.

Paul's desire to connect with people from different cultures and various expressions of religion was both beautiful and uncommon for people of his religious background. Yet, his passion to reach across boundaries was not totally selfless and sincere as he had an ulterior motive... *"to save some"* or to convert them to be followers of Christ. So, Paul's connecting point can be seen as a set up or a call to repentance and salvation. Our motive and motivation to connect with a diverse group of people should be that we are all people. We all breathe the same air, drink the same water. We are all warmed by the same sun and gaze into the same sky. We are all eternal spiritual beings having a temporary human experience and expression. We do not connect with other humans to sell anything, not even Jesus. We connect to bring comfort and encouragement. And in this way, we allow each person we touch to sense Christ in us.

Prayer: *"God of All, enable me to become all things to all people in order to share Your love and light without an agenda. Amen."*

Send Me What I Need

11/18/21

Affirmation

"The Universe will send to me whatever I need for the evolution of my consciousness. I am open and available for this growth and unfoldment...however it finds its way to me."

Hidden things unexpectedly find their way to the surface every day and in various ways. Occasionally, situations arise in our lives that seem to be unfair and even strange. Yet, we can be at peace knowing that even the most bizarre and challenging seasons carry with them a lesson and a wisdom that possess the potential to emancipate us from mental stagnation, force us to rethink and elevate us into our higher and highest selves. The Apostle Paul spoke of a *"thorn in his flesh"* that was used by God to enable him to receive and relay deep revelations and unrevealed mysteries. Jesus was *"driven into the wilderness by the Spirit to be tempted by the devil"* and afterward returned with great power and a new authority. Peter was stuck in religious bondage and mired in prejudicial perceptions of other cultures. So, God put him into a deep sleep and sent him a vision regarding his need to be more open and inclusive.

Every day, I experience something new that is designed for the evolution of my consciousness. I also observe this process happening in those around me. The racially prejudiced father has a daughter who marries someone of another race. A homophobic mother must come to grips with the reality of having a gay son. A male chauvinist must learn to work for a powerful female boss. A religious zealot finds a new friendship with someone who believes differently. All of these scenarios are the Universe's way of letting us know that we are loved, supported and cared for in an interconnected and interactive way that demands us to expand, unfold and evolve.

Prayer: *"Universe, send me whatever I need for the evolution of my soul. I don't want to be stuck, stale or stagnant. I relinquish my resistance and surrender to the lessons and wisdom You send my way. Amen."*

As Above, So Below

11/19/21

Affirmation

"Today, I will be aware that my outer world is only a reflection, and a manifestation, of my inner world. My thoughts are seeds. My life is the fruit. And today, I will reap a healthy harvest from positive, powerful thoughts."

Universal truth is never limited to one religion or region, one teacher or testament, one person or philosophy, one area or era. If it is timeless truth, it will survive and flourish as it finds its way into the hearts and minds of eager learners and hungry spirits throughout history everywhere. It may be said a little differently, but the message is the same:

"As a man thinks in his heart, so is he." -Proverbs 23:7
"As above, so below. As within, so without." -Hermes
"All we are is the result of what we have thought." -Buddha
"Let Your kingdom come…on earth as it is in heaven." -Jesus

This timeless truth, taught by diverse sages in different ages, is leading all of its adherents to the same place…within! Jesus said it beautifully, *"Let Your kingdom come, let Your will be done, on earth (in manifestation) as it is in heaven (in imagination)."* Heaven, or the kingdom of God, is not a place, but a space…a space in thought. The earth represents the material world. Or better, the earth becomes the outer experience or our inner expression. The earth is an outer harvest of our inner planting. Our thoughts are seeds. And, we can either grow flowers or weeds. We create our lives from our thoughts. Our thoughts become vibrations that both attract things to us and repel other things away from us. Spiritual teacher Esther Hicks always reminds us that *"We are vibrational beings in a vibrational universe."* Set your intention today to purposefully plant thought-seeds that will yield a harvest of peace, power and prosperity.

Prayer: *"First Thought, let Your kingdom come in my manifestation as it is in my imagination. Amen."*

11/20/2021

Nothing New Under The Sun

Affirmation

"Today, I affirm that God lives without timelines and above linear thinking. The Alpha and Omega, the First and the Last, the Beginning and the End, He who Was, and Is, and Is To Come exists continually, eternally, in eternity. Yet, allows me to awaken in time."

History repeats itself. For me. For you. For us. Whether it is sideburns and bell-bottoms, or one country (or religion) attempting genocide (in the name of God) against another, look deeply enough and you will see a discernable, definable, distinct historical pattern repeating itself. Thus, "Nothing New Under the Sun." And, this pattern repeats itself to give us a second chance at a first opportunity. King Solomon lays this wisdom out for us…

"That which is has already been, And what is to be has already been; And God requires an account of what is past" (Ecclesiastes 3:15). The Amplified Bible's translation of this verse says, *"God seeks what has passed by [so that history repeats itself]."*

Humanities way of seeing history is usually limited to time and timelines. We think linearly. Yet, God is not linear. God is timeless. Cyclical. Said scientifically, energy is neither created nor destroyed. Said colloquially, what goes around comes around. What does this mean? God, in His, in Her, in "Its" timeless infinite cyclical existence, causes history to repeat itself so that we have several chances to learn lessons we could have, and possibly should have, learned the first time. Historical patterns of war, prejudice, discrimination, homophobia, xenophobia, religi-phobia, are all cyclically, painfully, predictably and even graciously repeating in the hopes that we will finally "get it." So, history is not only repeating. History is repeating for you! Give thanks. There is a historically repeating lesson for you to learn today.

Prayer: *"Infinite Wisdom, thank You for causing history to repeat and for offering me another opportunity to 'get it.' I will! Amen."*

11/21/2021

Bless It Coming. Bless It Going.

Affirmation

"Today, I will remember not to block any blessing coming my way by closing my heart or my hands. I will allow blessings to flow to me and then through me. My mind is the channel through which good things come to me. As good things flow to me, I will hold them loosely, enjoy them as long as they are positive, purposeful and productive, and then know when to graciously release them. I am confident that the same Source who sent one blessing my way has many more in store."

The musical group 38 Special wrote a song titled *"Hold on loosely."* The lyrics hold quite a wealth of wisdom, *"Just hold on loosely, but don't let go. If you cling too tightly, you're gonna lose control."* I resonate with most of this philosophy. When we cling too tightly, to money, to relationships, to things and become overly possessive or hyper protective, we unconsciously operate in a vibration of lack and a spirit of fear.

Sometimes we have to let go, release and rest assured that just as we celebrate new friends who come into our lives we may have to release them at some point. When we learn to bless and release we safeguard our minds against any bitterness that may clog up the conduit through which other blessings are trying to flow to us and through us. Friends, jobs, things, even thoughts…bless them all coming and going. Our minds are channels, portals, receptors. And, we can either keep our pipes clean and our plumbing clear or we can allow them to get stopped up with fear and backed up with resentment. How we end or release one season determines how we begin the next season. All highways connect to another. Streams flow to rivers and rivers connect to the ocean. And, one season of our lives is connected to the next. When a new season arrives, bless it. When it fades, release it. And, watch what happens when you remain open.

Prayer: *"Ever-Flowing Source, today I will celebrate new blessings and gladly release them knowing they flow to me and through me. Amen."*

Day 61

11/22/2021

Worshipping in Spirit and in Truth

Affirmation

"I affirm that God is bigger than any religion, yet visits and can be occasionally discovered in most of them. I acknowledge that the fullness of God cannot be contained in any one holy book, confined to any one specific religion or defined by any one leader. God is not partial to location, sanctuary, temple or mosque, but is equally present in all of creation at all times. God is Spirit. And today, I will worship in Spirit and in Truth."

Jesus is such an amazingly complex figure. At one point on His journey He told a Canaanite woman that He wouldn't help her or her daughter and informed her He wasn't even sent to help her or her people...who were dogs...yikes (Matthew 15:21-26). On another occasion, at Jacob's well, He engages a Samaritan woman in a conversation challenging her to see God as being bigger than any culture, impartial to any geographical location and unconcerned with religion (John 4:1-26). We can take comfort in knowing that as Jesus *"grew in grace and truth"* (Luke 2:40), so will we. And, as Jesus was *"perfected"* (Hebrews 5:9), we will be too. Like Jesus, we too will eventually ascend from the tribalism of cultural bias and overcome religious exclusivism. We will one day be able to worship Father God, Mother God, in Spirit and in Truth. And, pave the way for others to do the same.

A key point in this conversation is when Jesus tells the Samaritan woman that He is not coming to worship on her mountain and doesn't need to drag her back to His temple. After this declaration He explains why. He tells her that God is Spirit, and desires to be, or must be, worshipped in Spirit and in Truth. Jesus paints the picture that God is actively seeking worshippers who understand this spiritual truth. If God is Spirit, then God is neither male nor female. God is not a Christian or a Muslim. God is not an American or a Mexican. God is not a Democrat or a Republican. God is Spirit.

Prayer: *"God As Spirit, I worship You without the boundary of culture or bondage of religion. I worship You in Spirit and in Truth. Amen."*

11/23/2021

No Secret Thoughts

Affirmation

"I am aware that I create my life with my thoughts. My private, secret thoughts show up in my life and as my life. Nothing remains hidden. And in essence, my life becomes a looking glass for everyone to see what I have been thinking."

As we begin to understand the creative power of our thoughts, we also notice that they do indeed show up as our reality and our experience of life. It may seem like a negative, a warning or maybe even a threat, the idea that our secret thoughts show up as our lives. On the contrary, our thoughts are not displayed publicly with the intention of embarrassing or humiliating us. Our secrets surface to engage us fully in the process of self-awareness, "knowing thyself" and fully awakening to our divine potential and god-like power to create, and hopefully, re-create our lives.

What Job "feared the most" came upon him and surfaced as his life. Peter, secretly struggling in his commitment and loyalty to Jesus, denied Him just as Jesus predicted. Paul, privately burdened with his bias toward women, manifests a doctrine that women should remain silent in church and even encourages some of his male disciples to reconsider the necessity of marriage. David, privately desiring Uriah's wife, Bathsheba, manifests his lustful thoughts, destroys another man's life and almost his own. All of these are difficult and hurtful moments…embarrassing. Yet, none of these and other scenarios of public revelations are intended for our or anyone's humiliation or devastation. Our thoughts come to the surface and manifest because the Universe desires for us to be transformed, to be self-actualized and to become fully awake. And, the Universe will faithfully and frequently send to us whatever is necessary for the evolution of our consciousness and for the maturation of the goodness and god-ness within us.

Prayer: *"Universal Mind, thank you for the opportunity to see myself and for the chance to fully own the creative power of my thoughts. Amen."*

11/25/2021

Empty Your Cup

Affirmation

"Today, I am willing to empty my cup, clear my mind, release old wine and ancient wineskins that would keep me from hearing and receiving what the Spirit is saying. I am willing to detach from the known and be open to the unknown. I have heard of old, but I am willing to hear today."

There is a common story in Buddhism of a young scholar seeking wisdom from an older Zen master. The young scholar sits with the master and goes on and on of his understanding of Zen. As he talks, the older master begins to pour him a cup of tea. When the tea reaches the top of the cup he continues to pour and even allows the tea to spill everywhere. The young scholar tells the master that he is spilling and that the cup cannot hold anymore tea. The old master says to the young scholar, *"You are like this cup. You ask for teaching but your cup is full. Before I can teach you, you must empty your cup."*

The most famous martial artist of my generation, Bruce Lee, used this philosophy to create a new and more advanced form of martial arts. Many martial arts purists did not believe you could combine new moves and unknown maneuvers with the old trusted methods. Their cups were completely full and there was no room for anything new. When criticized by these traditionalists, Bruce Lee said to them, *"Empty your cup so that it may be filled; become devoid to gain totality."* Every off season, Kobe Bryant, 5 time NBA champion, NBA MVP and top 5 scoring leader in NBA history, decided to learn new moves. Tiger Woods, arguably the greatest golfer of all time, continues to tweak his swing. The Apostle Paul described this philosophy as *"counting it all loss"* and admitting that he had *"not yet attained."* Jesus encourages us to become like little children. Experts become masters as they remain open and continually make the choice to empty their cups.

Prayer: *"Eternal Word, I empty my cup, celebrate the Beginner's Mind and make room for more. I will empty my cup. Fill my cup Lord! Amen."*

11/26/2021

The Sin Against the Holy Spirit

Affirmation

"Today, I will welcome the Holy Spirit into my life by allowing It to have Its way. I am open to hearing all truth, even the truth of myself. I am aware that the Holy Spirit has been sent to me to lead me into all truth. I will not restrict It from operating in my life by declaring that I already have all truth."

I was raised with an abiding and ever-present fear that I would sin against the Holy Spirit. Jesus taught that if we did sin against the Holy Spirit, it would be an unforgiveable sin. Needless to say, as a preacher's kid, I was leery of "playing church" or pretending that I was speaking in tongues as I perceived this might be sinning against the Holy Spirit. As I grew in knowledge and had experiences with the presence of the Holy Spirit I began to open up to a greater understanding. Not only did I sense the presence of the Holy Spirit, I began to receive new revelations and awaken to deep mysteries I had never known or heard before. I realized the purpose of the Holy Spirit in my life was to guide me into green pastures, new ideas and hidden truths of spirituality, and of myself.

It came to me, if the Holy Spirit was sent to guide me into all truth, then the sin against the Holy Spirit was not playing church. The sin against the Holy Spirit was perceiving that I already had all truth. I began to say things like "I don't know." Amazingly, as I detached from the known, a steady knowing flooded my daily experience. As I allowed the Holy Spirit to operate fully by creating space in my mind, new thoughts and quantum revelations became common place. Further, I realized that sinning against the Holy Spirit was only unforgivable, not because God wouldn't or couldn't forgive it, but because a "know it all" doesn't possess the capacity to see the error of his "know-it-all-ness." Therefore, the condition cannot be changed, or "forgiven," because there is no awareness that there is a condition. Empty your cup, create space, and experience a constant flow of truth from the Holy Spirit.

Prayer: *"Holy Ghost, have Your way! I give You permission to guide me into all truth, this day and every day. Amen."*

11/26/2021

Freedom From Labels

Affirmation

"Today, I declare and celebrate my personal freedom from labels. No temporary label can define or confine my eternal spirit. I am bigger than any label of race, religion or region. I do not have a need to identify with any label and I also relinquish any right to label others. In Spirit, the only label I carry is love! I am the skinless, sinless, endless, nameless, shameless, blameless, label-less image and nature of God and good in the earth! I believe it! I perceive it. Now, I receive it!"

Before we took on physical form, we were spirit, without skin or sin, name or shame, region or religion, gender or geography. As we emerged into the physical, we took on many labels unconsciously: white, black, gay, straight, male, female, American, Christian, etc. Then, we permitted this labeling to condition us to believe we were inherently different and eventually, inevitably, separate from the rest of the world and especially different from anyone who didn't carry our specific set of labels. Humanity's inability, or unwillingness, to relinquish labels is the reason we fear terrorism, nuclear annihilation and the prospect of race wars. Labels lead to otherness. Otherness leads to separation. Separation leads to intolerance. And, intolerance leads to violence. It all begins with a seemingly innocent label.

There is a higher law, a more perfect way. As Sting says, "*There is a deeper wave than this.*" And, as Paul explains to the Galatians and Colossians, in the renewed Christ mind, where there are no labels, "*there is neither male nor female, Greek nor Jew, circumcised nor uncircumcised, barbarian, Scythian, slave nor free, but all are one in Christ.*"

Prayer: *"God Without Label, awaken me to never be defined, disqualified or dismissed by any label. The only label I carry, or care about, is Spirit! Protect my love, preserve my life and promote my light without the bondage of any label. Help me today. I want to live without limit, purely in love and completely above label... just like You. Amen."*

11/27/2021

My Happy Place

Affirmation

"Today, I choose to be happy. I believe I deserve to be happy. And, I am actively seeking my happy place as my eyes, ears and mouth are only open to information that will bring happiness to me and through me. I will choose my words, my thoughts, my deeds and my friends wisely...making sure they are all in harmony with who I am."

Everyone wants happiness. Everyone desires to be at peace. Miss America knows to talk about world peace. But, what are the choices we make every day to make peace and create happiness in our lives? There are several ways we create happiness. Consciously, and unapologetically, choose to be around happy people. It takes an immense amount of mental strength to maintain happiness when you spend your time around unhappy people. Unhappy people never find happiness and don't want you to. Even on the occasion that happiness finds them or when good things unexpectedly arise, unhappy people will inevitably find a way to be skeptical, unimpressed and cast a sarcastic, negative light on everything good.

It sounds simple, but often some of the negative people of lower vibration are our family members. Release the guilt. Win the battle over obligation. And, spend your time around people of high energy and good vibrations. Once you establish your circle of friends, filter the information that comes your way. There is always a "Debbie downer" lurking in the shadows waiting for the first opportunity to bring you the news and gossip of the day and to convince you the glass is indeed half empty. Be courteous and gracious. Then, end the conversation as quickly as possible. These people are energy thieves. Misery loves company. Don't align yourself with people who feel their calling is to be the bearer of bad news. Choose happiness today. Choose to be around happy people. Filter the information coming your way. Get happy, stay happy, and see what happens!

Prayer: *"God of Joy, I know that Your joy is my strength. Today, I will protect my joy by guarding my heart, mind, ears and mouth. Amen."*

Day 67

Get Off My Ship

Affirmation

"Today, I will be conscious of who is on my ship, how they influence my direction and ultimately determine my destination. I will trust that the same Spirit guiding me toward my destiny is also ordering the steps of others. I will release those not destined to ride with me and rest in the knowledge that the same God who is perfecting those things concerning me is actively making a way for all of His children."

In the story of Jonah, he is commanded by God to go to Nineveh (Mosul, Iraq). Instead, he chooses to disobey and boards a ship headed for Tarshish (Lebanon). So, Jonah is going the wrong way. And, the ship heading toward their appointed arrival is carrying a passenger, Jonah, who will eventually detour their direction and distract from their destiny. Not long after their departure, the ship encounters an epic storm. Jonah informs the other passengers that he is the reason for the storm and insists they should throw him off of the ship. They refuse to throw Jonah overboard and instead being to throw everything else imaginable into the sea in the hopes that they will satisfy the anger of the storm. Finally, as a last resort, they put Jonah off of the ship. Immediately, the storm subsides, the ship makes it safely to Tarshish and then God provides Jonah transportation to Nineveh via the help of a large fish.

It may seem cruel, throwing Jonah off of the ship and into the turbulent stormy waters. Yet, Jonah got to his designed destination. Further, the ship survived the storm and arrived at its intended port. However, had they stayed connected to each neither would have survived. Are you on the wrong ship? Are you carrying the wrong person on your ship? Trust that God desires everyone involved to fulfill their purpose and disconnect, give it to God and watch as things fall into place.

Prayer: *"Captain of the Sea, give me the wisdom to board the right ship and the courage to carry the right passengers. Amen."*

11/29/2024

Laughing in Difficult Moments

Affirmation

"Today, I will laugh, even in difficult moments, knowing there is a joy set before me. I will surrender to joy and grant laughter permission to soothe my soul, settle my mind, secure my sanity and solidify my serenity. I am persuaded by the truth that all things are working together for my good. And today, my face will reflect my belief."

Growing up I was conditioned to believe that seriousness was equivalent to spirituality, sadness was sacred and a scowl was synonymous with sincerity. My childhood friends and I actually referred to this cultural religiosity as having a "stinky prophet face." Catching a prophet smiling or capturing a pastor laughing was like seeing an endangered species awkwardly roaming around in a busy urban area. Religious leaders laughing, enjoying life and letting their hair down was quite a rare treat and almost made them seem real to us…even human. It took me years to overcome this dysfunctional conditioning. I refused the burden of carrying around a "pain body" in order to prove my commitment to God and others, and to be found "worthy" of my own personal calling.

Before I had broken free of this philosophy, I was a young man, 19 years old, and my world began to crumble around me. I approached this storm with what I had always seen…seriousness, sanctity and sadness. As a result, I almost had an emotional and nervous breakdown…as a teenager. A decade later, I was married, a father of two, and had founded my own church. My world was shaken again. But, this time, I chose to laugh, love and live my life while navigating a ferocious storm that would have overwhelmed me otherwise. I emerged from the storm, happy, healthy and headed toward peace and prosperity. There is an old adage, "A ship can sail through any storm, as long as the storm doesn't get in the ship." Never lose your laughter. It may be the very thing that carries you safely through deadly storms and difficult seasons.

Prayer: *"Sacred Laughter, I honor you as a welcomed guest. Thank you for keeping me strong, serene, safe and sane through life's storms. Amen."*

11/30/21

At Peace With My Journey

Affirmation

"Today, I am at peace with my journey. Spirit has revealed truth to me line upon line; unlocked mysteries through me precept upon precept; transformed me from glory to glory and transitioned me from one dimension to another. I am not where I was. I am not where I will be. However, I am at peace with where I am. And, I am open to whatever is next."

I have a friend who says, "Christians are a lot like concrete…all mixed up and permanently set." I have witnessed the epidemic of this mental stagnation and spiritual constipation for most of my life. For some reason, we have a strong tendency to find a truth, cherish it, protect it, cling to it and then in an attempt to preserve it, refuse to make room for more truth. Like good soldiers, we stubbornly march with loyalty to what God said while resisting the guilt, and perceived gluttony, of cheating on the last word from God by dating the new or next word. There is a pattern in the Bible, from Genesis to Revelation, of God revealing and unfolding a little more truth each step of the way. While in the wilderness, the Hebrew children ate manna each morning. This mysterious food would only last one day. Each day there was new, fresh, organic food. There is a *"Daily Bread,"* a *"Living Word"* available to us each day as long as we are at peace with the constant transformation. Jesus made it clear, *"Man shall not live by bread alone, but by each word that proceeds from the mouth of God"* (Matthew 4:4). The word "proceeds" is an active verb found in the present tense. In other words, it is always happening…God is always speaking.

The truth that fed you in the last season may sustain you in this one. You can survive on it. But, you are filling your spirit with preservatives, leftovers. Give thanks for yesterday's truth. They are not gravestones to be mourned. They are stepping stones of gratitude and graduation. And, don't throw out the baby with the bathwater. Eat what is eternal. Edit what is temporary. Enjoy the new.

Prayer: *"Proceeding Word, I give thanks for where You have brought me from. And, I trust where You are taking me to. Amen."*

12/1/21

I Am Not My Beliefs

Affirmation

"Through this awakening process I have realized I am not my beliefs. I am a spirit capable of considering, having and even changing beliefs. I am at peace being surrendered to the process of the Holy Spirit guiding me into all truth, even if all truth is different from my present truth."

Christ may be a Solid Rock on which we can stand, but His journey toward higher truth was fluid. The strength of Jesus is hidden away, not in His rigidity, but in His flexibility. On one occasion He attempted to teach a rigid, inflexible religious leader named Nicodemus the recipe for spirituality:

> *"That which is born of the flesh is flesh, and that which is born of the Spirit is spirit. Do not marvel that I said to you, 'You must be born again.' The wind blows where it wishes, and you hear the sound of it, but cannot tell where it comes from and where it goes. So is everyone who is born of the Spirit."* (John 3:6-8).

This doesn't mean we are to be *"blown about by every wind of doctrine"* (Ephesians 4:14). It does mean we must not be so stuck in what God has said that we miss what God is saying. Many times Jesus would begin a teaching by saying, *"You have heard it was said of old, but I say to you."* Those weakened by loyalty to what was said could not summon the strength to hear what God was saying. We must be cognizant that faith comes by hearing, not by having heard.

The tallest buildings in major cities are built with a flexible design. These skyscrapers actually sway back and forth with the wind. Palm trees, planted by shorelines that are regularly visited by hurricanes and heavy winds, can literally bend over and touch the ground without breaking. Whether it is a building, a tree, our bodies, or our spirits, flexibility signals strength while rigidity invites weakness.

Prayer: *"Wind of the Spirit, I am not fragile. I am flexible. I invite You to blow truth to me and through me. I can handle it. Amen."*

12/2/2021

Divine Connections

Affirmation

"Today, I am open and available for Divine Connections. I welcome relationships that bless me with loyalty, honesty, inspiration, vision and power. I will be receptive when a Divine Connection speaks a divine correction or difficult truth to me. And, I will be grateful when a Divine Connection affirms who I am."

Have you ever met someone and immediately had a strong sense that you had known this person your entire life? Or maybe even in another lifetime? Meetings like this are divinely appointed as they are Divine Connections. Said differently, the vibration you send out will attract people to you who operate from the same vibratory pattern and live on the same frequency. Once you tap into that wavelength, you begin to channel people of like minds. Most of us have family, friends and acquaintances we have known for a lifetime, and yet, have never felt as closely connected to them as we do to a Divine Connection we have known for a few hours. The defense mechanisms in us seem to resist giving in fully to these newly discovered Divine Connections as we are programmed to protect our hearts and are trained to be leery of trusting a stranger that we have only just met. There is nothing wrong with these protective measures as we have learned to trust in them to keep us safe. And, a truly Divine Connection will not be scared off by any sense of hesitancy. What God has joined cannot be separated.

Divine Connections offer us a powerful opportunity to grow, give and gain deeper understandings of others, ourselves and the nature of who we truly are, and are becoming. Divine Connections bless us with revelation, elevation, motivation and occasionally correction. When a Divine Connection humbly offers a divine correction, don't be offended or afraid. Digest it and give thanks for someone the Universe has sent to help protect you from yourself and any potential blind-spots.

Prayer: *"Divine Connection, thank You for every Divine Connection. I give thanks for connection and remain open for correction. Amen."*

12/3/21

We Don't Get What We Want. We Get Who We Are.

Affirmation

"Vibration is happening around and through me at all times, whether I am aware of it or not. I know the truth, that I am a vibrational being in a vibrational universe. I am also awake to the universal law that I attract people, relationships, experiences, opportunities and things to myself according to my level of vibration."

We all want a loving spouse, loyal friends, obedient children, understanding co-workers and a gracious boss. The difficult truth is wanting something does not create it. We must learn to manifest our desires by shifting our thoughts and raising our vibration to match the level of what it is we want. Otherwise, we will continue to want things and be frustrated that we don't receive them.

We don't get what we want, we get who we are. This statement can either arouse a great deal of optimism and hope or become a heavy burden of guilt and despair. If our lives are full of loneliness, lack and disloyalty we are only experiencing the level of vibration we exist in or we are merely manifesting who we are in our daily lives.

"Birds of a feather flock together…" "Whatever we sow, that will we reap…" "The apple doesn't fall far from the tree…" "An object in motion stays in motion unless acted upon…" "Like tends toward like." These colloquial, religious, philosophical and even scientific sayings are all pointing us to the idea that we get who we are. This knowledge can cause a great deal of heaviness. However, instead of living in guilt and regret, which do not produce positive change, accept this truth, own what you are creating and who you are, and raise your level of vibration to shift who you are. Then, as you begin to like yourself, or who you are, you will notice that you attract who you are to yourself.

Prayer: *"Ultimate Reality, I will raise my vibration to righteousness, peace and joy and watch as all good things are attracted to me. Amen."*

Day 73

December 4, 2021

Loving Myself. Loving Others. Loving God.

Affirmation

"As I learn to love myself, I will be able to love others and then see the way to love God. I cannot give to others, or to God, what I do not possess myself. Today, I will love me, and then be able to give out to others from the love I have for myself."

In Sunday school I was taught to put God first, to put others second and to put myself last. I carried this idea for years. Then one day, I realized that it just didn't work. We cannot love others if we don't love ourselves. This foundational religious idea is actually in reverse order. We have to love ourselves first, then love others, then love God. Jesus asked a question, *"How can you love God who you have not seen? When you do not love your neighbor who you have seen?"* Jesus went on to remind us that the most important law was to *"Love God, and love your neighbor as yourself."* Every major world religion teaches some form of the Golden Rule: Do unto others what you would have them do unto you. The question we must wrestle with is this: if every religion teaches its followers to love their neighbor as they love themselves, why is it not working? Why are religions at war with each other? The answer is pretty simple. We cannot give what we do not have. Put plainly, we are loving others as we love ourselves. The problem is we don't love ourselves. Jesus realized this was an issue. He told us to love our neighbors as we love ourselves. Then, He discovered how little we love ourselves. So, He altered His original command and issued a new one, *"A new commandment I give to you, that you love one another; as I have loved you."* (John 13:34).

When you're taught your whole life that you're fallen, wretched, helpless, hopeless, sinful and shameful, it is difficult to love yourself. Tell yourself a different story about yourself today. You're made in the image and likeness of God and good. Believe it. And, watch as your love grows for others and for God.

Prayer: *"Loving Creator, grant me the courage to love myself so that I may love others and love You with my whole heart. Amen."*

December 9, 2021

Recognizing Destructive Patterns Quickly

Affirmation

"Today I choose to make the most of this lifetime by recognizing destructive patterns quickly. I am aware that destructive thoughts lead to destructive choices; destructive choices become destructive behaviors; and destructive behaviors invite, enable and create destruction in my life. As I begin to think new thoughts, I am also cultivating new choices, establishing new behaviors and walking down new paths."

One of my mentors shared a piece of wisdom with me while I was in high school that still haunts me today. He said, "Some people can learn by hearing or observing. Other people learn through experience. But, there are some people who only learn by way of tragedy." People who refuse to learn any other way than by tragedy have an inability and an unwillingness to recognize destructive patterns quickly. We have all headed down paths that were either dangerous, or at very least unproductive. Realizing this quickly is the way we avoid a lifetime of pain and resist detours that put our destinies on layaway. Our lives are all on a long trajectory. When we get off track, the quicker we shift our trajectory the less severe the course correction will be down the line. Getting off course without recognizing it, or refusing to yield to a course correction, can result in finding ourselves in another galaxy far, far away.

Jesus offered a course correction to the woman at the well, to the woman caught in adultery, to the rich young ruler, to Zacchaeus the tax collector, to the Pharisees and to many others. Some received it, made quick adjustments and found their way back to purposeful living. Others rejected His wisdom and continued down the path toward tragedy. Today, set your intention to be a quick learner and visualize yourself heading directly toward the realization of your full potential.

Prayer: *"Course Corrector, with Your help, I will recognize destructive patterns quickly, adjust and enjoy a happy and fulfilled life. Amen."*

Day 75

The Power Of I Am

Affirmation

"Today I am aware that only I can say 'I Am.' The world I create begins with 'I Am' so I will be mindful of what I attach to 'I Am.' My 'I Am' is more powerful than anyone's 'you are.' No one's 'you are' could ever create my life unless their 'you are' becomes my 'I Am.'"

Isn't it amazing that you are the only person who can say "I Am?" No other person can say "I Am" for you or even about you. The best others can do when speaking about you is use the words "you are." And, the beautiful truth is that when they say "you are" it has absolutely zero power over you. Throughout our entire earth journey people will say "you are" in an attempt to criticize, demean or diminish us. However, they will continue to be unsuccessful as long as their "you are" statements never become our "I Am" statements. God, the "I Am that I Am" models this for us when He refuses to give Moses any other words or names after "I Am." Never give your "I Am" power away to anyone else's definition about you or labelling of you. "I Am" is all you need to harness the power of your divine creativity. And, "I Am" is yours and only yours.

You are made in the image and likeness of God. This means, you are not dependent on anyone or anything outside of yourself to create for you. Your "I Am" does not wait on anyone, blame anything or even ask permission. "I Am" is now. Once you awaken to the power of your "I Am" you will become more mindful not to project any negative "you are" statements onto others. You will especially not project "you are" onto God, the "I AM that I AM!" Sticks and stones may break our bones, but words will never hurt us…unless, those words become our beliefs. Negative people use negative words. Let them talk. Their opinion of you is none of your business. All that matters is what you think and say about yourself.

Prayer: *"Power of I Am, awaken me to the power my 'I Am.' Help me be aware of the power of my words about me. Amen."*

December 7, 2021

One Blood

Affirmation

"We are all the offspring of One Source…One Creator. And, we all share One Blood. Every country, culture and child must learn to coexist, cooperate and then celebrate our contradictions, complexities and commonalities. And today, I am willing to be a light of love and interconnectedness shining into the darkness of fear and separation. Whether we are Caribbean or Canadian, African or Anglo, we can live, move and have our being and becoming in the Christ Mind where there are no cultural boundaries separating God's creation. Today, I declare I am One Blood with all of humanity."

In 1980, the Jacksons released the song "Can You Feel It." The words are so powerful we actually sing this secular song at our church:

"All the children of the world should be, Loving each other wholeheartedly. Yes, it's all right, Take my message to your brother and tell him twice. Take the news to the marching men, Who are killing their brothers, when death won't do. Cause we're all the same, Yes, the blood inside me is inside of you."

Can you feel it? Not just the beat (which is really good). Can you feel the message in these lyrics? We all share the same blood. The blood flowing in your veins is the same as mine. People of different races can actually donate blood to each other. The blood being shed on battle fields is all the same blood, no matter which side we are on or which country or government we fight for. All the children of the world, the global human family, come from One Blood.

The Jacksons didn't create this idea, they borrowed it from the book of Acts:

"And He has made from One Blood every nation of men to dwell on all the face of the earth." (Acts 17:26).

Prayer: *"One Source, today I am aware that I share the same blood with all of Your creation. Let me be a symbol of harmony. Amen."*

Day 77

Your Appointed Time

Affirmation

"My appointed time is not some moment in the future. And, I have not missed my appointed time somewhere in my past. My appointed time is NOW! This is the day the Lord has made. Today is the day of salvation. There is no thing, and no one, to wait on. This is my appointed time. I believe it. I perceive it. And now, I receive it."

There is a generally accepted idea in many religious and denominational circles that God has specific seasons of favor, changes moods and says "yes" sometimes and "no" at other times. God does not have favorite people, favored times or even seasons of favor. Your appointed time and your season of favor is always now…whenever you awaken to your divine creativity and godlike capacity to think, speak and manifest the experience of life you desire by finding the vibration that yields that reality to you. The biggest threat, and greatest hindrance, to the kingdom of God coming among us is that it's somehow always on the way…not here now…waiting for appointed times and prophetic utterances to be fulfilled. Jesus taught that the kingdom of God is right now, not on the way or in the future:

> *"Now when He was asked by the Pharisees when the kingdom of God would come, He answered them and said, "The kingdom of God does not come with observation; nor will they say, 'See here!' or 'See there!' For indeed, the kingdom of God is within you"* (Luke 17:20-21).

Religious minds always get bogged down in the literal and miss the spiritual... unconsciously they give their creative power away to illusions of time and delusions of favor. There is nothing to wait on. God exists in eternity and doesn't submit to time. Be powerful by not giving your power away. Today is your appointed time. Now is where favor can be found.

Prayer: *"Timeless God, I give thanks that this is my appointed time. Today is my season of favor. Now is my moment. Amen."*

December 9, 2021

Christ Is All, and In All

Affirmation

"Today, I will be open to seeing Christ in all of creation. I will even allow myself to recognize Christ outside of the boundaries of Christianity. I am willing to see the Christ in me and in others. I will be awake today to the truth that Christ is all, and in all."

If all of creation came from God (or the Word of God), then all of creation carries the DNA of God. We find out in the first chapter of Genesis that we are made *"in the image and likeness of God."* So, *"Christ in us…the hope of glory"* is not something to be acquired. Christ is already in us…in all of creation. Christ in us is something to be uncovered and discovered within us. The Apostle Paul was speaking to the Colossian church about this idea of Christ being present in all of creation and said it this way:

> *"…put on the new man who is renewed in knowledge according to the image of Him who created him, where there is neither Greek nor Jew, circumcised nor uncircumcised, barbarian, Scythian, slave nor free, but Christ is all and in all"* (Colossians 3:10-11).

When you understand the depth of this verse it opens our minds to what Paul was really saying. The new man is renewed in knowledge. What knowledge? The knowledge of the image of Him who created us! Wow! The barbarians and Scythians did not even have a definable alphabet. In other words, Paul was declaring that those who had never heard or read about Christ, had the Christ Spirit within them. So in essence, Paul was not preaching Christ to the Colossians, Barbarians and Scythians…he was preaching to the Christ already present in these people in an effort to wake it up. Once we wake up to the Christ in us, we begin to grant ourselves permission to recognize the Christ in other people and places.

> ***Prayer:*** *"Christ In All, give me confidence to see You in me, courage to see You in others and openness to see You everywhere. Amen."*

December 10, 2021

Temporary Containers

Affirmation

"I know that I am an eternal spirit having a temporary human experience. My body is not eternal and not who I am. My body is simply a container, or the temple, that houses my spirit... for now."

Water will always take the shape of its container. The container is not the water. The container is only the housing of the water. If you poured the same water into another container of a different shape, the water would, without hesitation, take the shape of the new container. No container could ever boast that it has trained the water or figured out the shape of water. Similarly, Spirit may be housed by many different containers. And, Spirit may even take the shape of a particular container. However, Spirit is not the container. Containers such as religions, holy books or religious buildings, are only containers. When Spirit is poured into them, It may take the shape of that specific religious container, but the container is not Spirit. It is just temporary housing for Spirit.

Water, or H20, can actually take on 3 different forms...liquid (water), solid (ice) and gas (steam). Whatever form it takes, it is still the same substance. No matter its shape, texture or temperature, it is still water. Consider that the same Spirit that was working in the container we call Jesus was also present in Mahatma Gandhi, Martin Luther King, Jr. and is working around, in, through and as us. It was all the same Spirit, called by different names, just being housed in different containers.

Be conscious not to value the container more than the Spirit. Paul described our bodies as *"tents"* or temporary housing. Containers such as human bodies, churches, temples, synagogues, mosques are all just facilitation or temporary housing for eternal, shapeless, boundless Spirit. Build your hopes on things eternal, not on temporary things that will eventually pass away.

Prayer: *"Shapeless Spirit, give me the vision to recognize You regardless of the shape You take or the container You inhabit. Amen."*

December 11, 2021

Stillness Speaks

Affirmation

"God has never given me, or His creation, the silent treatment. God is not childish or moody. There is a constant flow, a Living Word, a fresh manna, always coming from the mouth of God. However, there may be times when I am not hearing God or agreeing with God. And, there may be times when I am looking for God's voice everywhere except within. I will not allow circumstances or distractions to convince me that God is not speaking to me. Instead, I will learn to be still and get quiet long enough to connect to the voice of God within me."

The book of Malachi was written somewhere around 400-450 B.C.E. Malachi is the last book of the Old Testament. The first Gospel of the New Testament, Mark, was written somewhere between 70-110 C.E. This gap between Malachi and Mark (over 400 years) is believed by most Christians to be a silent period where God was not speaking or even refused to speak. Years ago, I actually preached sermons promoting this idea and explaining that God wouldn't speak again until people heard the last thing He said. Whatever my justification, I am now awake to the truth that God does not give us the silent treatment.

Sometimes we don't hear the voice of God because It is not screaming at us. The voice of God within us is many times like a *"still small voice"* whispering to us and giving us impressions, intuitions and "knowings" within our hearts. Other times there is simply too much background noise, mindless chatter, family drama, work stress or busy-work drowning out the sound of God's voice. In environments like this, we could benefit tremendously from moments of stillness and uninterrupted quietness.

"Be still and know that I am God" (Psalm 46:10).
"In quietness...will be your strength" (Isaiah 30:15).

Prayer: *"Still Small Voice, today I will get still, quiet, surrender, connect, breathe, sense and hear Your voice within me. Amen."*

Dacember 12, 2021

A Double Portion

Affirmation

"Today, I welcome a double portion in my life by giving thanks for the positive and the negative. I will not be blinded by denial or burdened with delusion. Instead, I will endeavor to be fully awake, strive to repeat successes and remain open to learn from any missteps."

There is a story in the Bible of an older prophet, Elijah, mentoring a younger prophet, Elisha. As Elijah reaches the end of his life he asks Elisha what he wants him to do for him before he dies. Elisha answers, *"I want a double portion of your spirit."* Elijah replies, you'll have the double portion *"If you see me when I go."* On the surface, this seems pretty simple. If Elisha remains loyal and subservient to Elijah, stays by Elijah's side and is physically there when he transitions, Elisha will receive the double portion. This interaction has been skewed and twisted to embolden older leaders to manipulate younger leaders into inordinate and undying loyalty for generations. Elisha actually ended up performing twice the recorded miracles than that of Elijah. However, the mystery of the double portion is deeper than tallying miracles.

The mystery is hidden in Elijah's words, *"If you SEE ME when I go."* Elijah was a powerful prophet. Yet, he was burdened with imbalance, rage and fear. One day, he is cutting off the heads of 400 false prophets. The next day, he is running scared, hiding from a woman. Elisha's receiving of the double portion relied upon his willingness to see all of Elijah…good, bad, strength, weakness, spirit, flesh…all of it. Most of us are blessed with mentors who assist us on our journey. Sadly, most mentees become either highly critical of, or blindly loyal to, their mentors. The result of this imbalance is receiving only a single portion. Yet, the double portion exists in the middle; being fully able to give thanks for strengths while remaining completely open to see weaknesses. Review it all. Rest in the middle. Repeat the good. Refuse the bad. Receive the double portion.

Prayer: *"Awakened Vision, grant me a double portion. Give me eyes to see it, openness to survey it and courage to shift it. Amen."*

Flattery and Criticism

Affirmation

"Today, I will wear people's flattery, and their criticism, like a loose garment. Their flatteries touch me, but they do not cling to me. I feel their criticisms, but they don't restrict my movement. I will navigate them all while remaining fully awake."

Whether we want to or not, we all deal with criticism. Occasionally, criticism comes from a cherished friend or caring loved who deeply cares for us and wants us to grow into our highest and greatest good. Nothing to fear here. Give thanks for it and ask the Holy Spirit to help you apply what is useful. Other times, criticism comes from a mean-spirited competitive enemy disguised in friendly clothing. Sneakily, people use criticism to prey on our insecurities and gain our ear as some sort of needed guide coaching us with tough love into their picture of who we should become.

Flattery is a little more deceptive as it goes down more smoothly. Criticism is a jagged pill, difficult to swallow. Flattery is a subtle intoxicant, lulling us into places, and aligning us with people, we would have never considered while sober. Flattery feeds the veracious ego and offers us what we're hungering for. And, then exposes the predictable, tolerable daily routines with our loving families and trusted friends, that may lack a daily "blowing smoke up your skirt" session. I have watched criticism stymie powerful people. And, I have witnessed it save people's lives, marriages, business and callings. I have watched flattery destroy good-hearted preachers and crush innocent-minded parishioners. Wear all of it like a loose garment. It's touching you, but not tethering you. It's close, but not clingy. Allow it to be respectfully purposeful, without become restrictively paralyzing. And, when either comes your way, take a self-inventory of your own weaknesses and insecurities, and be sure a wolf in sheep's clothing is not preying on you.

Prayer: *"Protective Intuition, alert me to hateful criticism and alarm me to harmful flattery. Today, I need Your help and protection. Amen."*

 Dcember 14, 2021

I Walk Down A Different Street

Affirmation

> *"Chapter One of My Life: I walk down the street. There's a deep hole in the sidewalk. I fall in. I am lost. I am helpless. It isn't my fault. It takes forever to find a way out. Chapter Two: I walk down the same street. There's a deep hole in the sidewalk. I pretend I don't see it. I fall in again. I can't believe I'm in the same place! But it isn't my fault. And, it still takes a long time to get out. Chapter Three: I walk down the same street. There's a deep hole in the sidewalk. I see it there. I still fall in. It's a habit! My eyes are open. I know where I am. It is my fault. I get out immediately. Chapter Four: I walk down the same street. There's a deep hole in the sidewalk. I walk around it. Chapter Five: I walk down a different street." (Portia Nelson, There's a Hole In My Sidewalk: The Romance of Self-Discovery)."*

I used this short story as our affirmation today because it has powerfully impacted my life and confirmed so much in regards to channeling power and divine creativity. It is a quick journey and quantum leap from being a victim to becoming a victor. See if you can critically follow the evolution and elevation.

Chapter One begins with ignorance, powerlessness, shame and blame. Chapter Two continues with the same ingredients, but by adding dash of denial. Chapter Three takes a powerful turn by awakening from denial, admitting there is a repeating pattern, owning it and then reaping the reward of a quicker recovery. Chapter Four is the fruitful progress and practical application of the knowledge gained in Chapter Three. Chapter Five is total and complete freedom from the past and the full awakening to what is possible when we own what we have created and then choose to re-create something better. Sometimes in life, we innocently and ignorantly create pain. However, the pain is the only teacher needed. The second time we feel the pain it signals our refusal to learn and evolve. The simple truth is that there is no learning from the second kick of a horse. See it, sense it, survey it, shift it and then settle on a new street.

Prayer: *"God of the Second Chance, thank You for showing me the pitfalls on my street and for the courage to choose a new street. Amen."*

Eating The Question

Affirmation

"Today, I will relax into the mystery. I will be at peace with the process of answering questions and questioning answers. I will celebrate truth as a journey, and not as a destination. And, I will eat the question knowing it may be my connecting point to a new dimension and a higher elevation."

The Hebrew children have been delivered out of the bondage of Egypt and rescued from 400 years of enslavement. They are now free. But, afraid, unsure, in a strange place and having to learn new ways of being and doing. They have a pillar of fire to warm them at night, a cloud to shade them from the heat of the day and water coming out of rocks to satisfy their thirst. Their food is also a mysterious provision. It is called "manna," which is more of a question than just a word. Manna means "what is it?" So in essence, each morning, in order to survive, they must eat the question. Similar to our journey toward liberation, there is a connecting flight between bondage and freedom. They departed from Egypt, had a layover in the wilderness, and eventually arrived in the Promised Land. But, in order to make it to the promise they were forced to eat the question.

What are the questions we are presented with as we connect from one season to another? Why did my marriage fail? Why don't my children respect me? Why am I always disappointed? Do I need more money or more money management? Who is to be blamed? Is it working for me? The questions can be many and not so easy to eat and digest. The Hebrews didn't particularly like eating the manna, the question. They asked Moses to take them back to Egypt, where they would be in bondage again, but also have bread, pots of meat and not have to eat the question. Yet, until they, and we, eat and digest the questions, we will continue to remain in the wilderness. This is our journey. Eat the questions or go back to bondage. Questions are answers in seed form. And, they hold the key to our Promised Land.

Prayer: *"Eternal Mystery, thank You for freeing me from the bondage of my past. Strengthen me to walk into freedom. Amen."*

December 16, 2021

4 Levels of Thought Progression

Affirmation

"I have the capacity to think on many different levels. When I was a child, I thought, spoke and processed information as a child. I existed on a lower level of conscious awareness. Today, I am willing to put away childish things and think on a higher plane."

There are many different levels of thought. In my journey, I describe them 4 different ways: Absolute, Abstract, Mystic Receptivity and Spiritual Oneness. Absolute thought is concrete thinking, cut and dry, black and white, no complexities, no questions and no room for discussion. "Brush your teeth." "Don't get near the street." "Why? Because I said so." In Abstract thought, we begin to see that truth may not be found in the extremes, but rather, held in the tension between extremes where absolute thought encounters contradiction, crisis, surrenders and is then introduced to grey areas. In Mystic Receptivity, we begin to get comfortable with contradiction. We choose to celebrate truth as a journey, not a destination. Questions become as, or more, important than answers. Finally, we arrive at Spiritual Oneness where the truth we have been searching for is amazingly discovered within us. The kingdom we are waiting on is within us. The God we are praying to is within us. We begin to see ourselves as the offspring of God and an extension, example and earthly expression of divinity. In Spiritual Oneness we begin to *"behold in the mirror the glory of God."* Spiritual Oneness requires a strong connection to self-government as the laws that bound us, and the punishments that scared us, no longer exist in this higher level of thinking. In Spiritual Oneness we don't beg or even ask. We begin to manifest the life we desire through an awareness that we are created by God, creative like God and creating as gods.

We all change, but at our own pace and in our own space. Wherever you are in thought progression, keep walking, pressing, listening, asking, growing.

Prayer: *"Higher Mind, elevate me to higher thought…from one progression to another. I am ready. Amen."*

December 17, 2021

The Power of Choice

Affirmation

"Today, I will exercise my power to choose. I choose to be around people of awakened minds and higher vibrations. I choose to be kind and not invest in relationships fueled by anger or angry people. I choose to be patient and not live my life around impatient people who make everything difficult. I choose to wake up to my divine creativity and to live a life not burdened with pity parties and blaming others for my lack of happiness."

There is a question that has been asked innumerable times by countless people: "Where did evil come from?" If God is good, and God created all things, did God create evil? This is a question that requires graduation from the lower levels of absolute thought. It is a complex answer. Our Creator created us like Him, Her, It. Which means we have the power to create. Most theologians refer to this as "free will" or the power of choice. With this power of choice, we can create love, peace and joy. Or, we can create hate, war and sorrow. The power of choice is not evil. And, it's actually not good. The power of choice is neutral with the potential to be used for good or evil. So, God did not create evil. God gave us the power to choose that carries with it the potential for good or evil. The real question is not: "did God create evil?" The question that will enlighten our minds, empower our journeys and enhance our lives is this: "why did God trust us with something that carries the potential for evil?" God gave us, trusted us, endowed us, with the power to choose because we are here to learn how to navigate our divine creativity. In other words, we are here to learn how to be like God.

That's a lot of theology for a daily affirmation. So, let's apply this knowledge to our daily lives. We are endowed by God, with the power to choose our friends, spouses, jobs, churches, foods, political candidates. We choose money or the environment, convenience or health, inclusion or exclusion, power or peace. We choose love or hate, fear or faith, joy or pain. Own and hone your power today. God trusted you with it.

Prayer: *"Giver of Freedom, help me choose life today. Amen."*

Day 87

December 18, 2021

Ending With the Beginning in Mind

Affirmation

"Today, I will position myself for success by ending this season the way I wish to begin the next. I will not waste time or energy predicting my future. Instead, I will create my future by agreeing to the process of transformation. I may not be exactly where I want to be. But, thank God I know I'm not where I used to be. There is a deposit of divinity anxiously waiting to be expressed through me. God desires to be God in, through and as me. And today, I will let God, be God, as me."

We have all heard motivational speeches for sports, education, fitness regimens, investing, that include the phrase, "Begin with the end in mind." In other words, begin a season the same way you want to end it. Today, we are looking at this idea, but in reverse, "End with the Beginning in Mind." In other words, end one season of your life as if the way you ended it determined the beginning of your next season. Let's go a little further. What if, in reality, there is no beginning or ending? What if it is all connected and continuous? Seasons, jobs, relationships…all of it, connected.

Life is not segmented into disparate, disconnected sections. All life is connected. If a butterfly in California can flap its wings and affect the weather patterns in Hawaii…you know the rest. This life philosophy is about more than just protecting our professional reputations so that former employers will give us good references when we want a new job. This is about setting up the conditions of our minds to emit an endless vibration that continually declares to the Universe that peace, possibility and prosperity are the order of the day. On a deeper level, if God is eternal, Alpha and Omega, First and Last, Beginning and Ending, then as we awaken to the idea that one season is connected to another season, that all of life is interconnected cyclically, not linearly, we begin to surrender to the truth that we are like God, divine, without beginning or ending. And, we open up a portal that empowers us to continually experience happiness and fulfillment.

Prayer: *"Beginning and Ending, I get it now. Thank You. Amen."*

Dicember 19, 2021

The Ever-Present Christ Presence

Affirmation

"Today, I affirm that the Christ Presence has always been in the world, even before Jesus was born. And, I am open to waking up to the Christ Presence, Principle, Power, Purpose and Person within me."

Most Christians would agree that Jesus of Nazareth is the Christ Person. But, is it possible that the Christ Presence was in the world before the Christ Person showed up? And, does the Christ Presence still exist in the world now? After Jesus ascended? I believe we find the Presence of Christ all throughout the Bible before the account of the birth of Jesus. Genesis 1:2 *"and the Spirit of God was hovering over the waters."* The Christ Presence was in the lion's den with Daniel, shutting the mouths of the lions. The Christ Presence was in the fiery furnace with the three Hebrew children. King Nebuchadnezzar looked into the furnace and said, *"Look! I see four men loose, walking in the midst of the fire; and they are not hurt, and the form of the fourth is like the Son of God"* (Daniel 3:25). Paul refers to a High Priest named Melchizedek (who lived around 2,000 B.C.E.) who was called the, *"king of righteousness," "king of peace,"* and who was *"without father, without mother, without genealogy, having neither beginning of days nor end of life, but made like the Son of God, remains a priest continually"* (Hebrews 7:2-3). Sound familiar? And Jesus, happens to be a priest according to the order of Melchizedek. Consider this key verse: *"And it is yet far more evident if, in the likeness of Melchizedek, there arises another priest who has come, not according to the law of a fleshly commandment, but according to the power of an endless life"* (Hebrews 7:15-16). Jesus is the other priest who arises in the likeness of Melchizedek.

What's the point? Christ was in the world before Jesus. Christ was in the world as Jesus. And, Christ is now in the world as you. Christ in you, Christ through you and Christ as you, is the hope of glory.

Prayer: *"Ever-Present Christ Presence, I acknowledge Your Eternal Presence in the world and working in me. Amen."*

December 20, 2024

The Walking Bible

Affirmation

"Today, I will be the hands of God extending to a hurting world. I will allow the Word to become flesh and dwell in me. I may not read the Bible to someone or inspire them to read it for themselves. But, I will be as a walking Bible, a living epistle, being read by all men and graciously offering God's love to all."

My grandfather was a preacher. A very unique one. His nickname was "The Walking Bible." On one occasion, a local journalist came to hear him speak and then wrote an article about the experience. The writer reported my grandfather had quoted over 300 different bible verses from memory during one sermon. When I would hear of my family referring to him as "The Walking Bible" I always understood it in this context…memorizing Bible verses. It wasn't until later that I had a deeper understanding that we all must become "The Walking Bible." This is not to suggest that we all commit to memory the entire Bible or even specific scriptures. It is to suggest that we are all "Walking Bibles" and should embrace and accept the truth that we are the only Bible some people will ever read.

Our love, our light and our lives are the only Bible some people will ever experience. Paul said we are *"living" and "written epistles…read by all men."* Our presence becomes the Bible. Our actions become the chapters. Our words become the verses. Our light must shine so brightly that it reflects the love of God in every environment we frequent. Preaching on a street corner takes courage, and a touch of crazy. However, the greatest sermon we could give is to become an extension of God's love in our daily relationships. There is an old saying that has become somewhat cliché, "People don't care how much you know, until they know how much you care." Talk the talk. Walk the walk. You are the Word become flesh.

Prayer: *"Living Word, let Your light wake in me, Your love work through me and Your Word walk as me. Let my walk be louder than my talk. Amen."*

December 21, 2021

Matrix, Mind, Mouth, Manifestation

Affirmation

"Life and death are in the power of how I see and say. My matrix processes it. My mind presents it. My mouth proclaims it. My manifestation produces it. Today, I will be aware of the matrix, mind, mouth, manifestation connection."

One of the most popular verses in the Bible is "*Death and life are in the power of the tongue*" (Proverbs 18:21). This verse assures us that the power is not in life or in death. The power is in the tongue. But, when we think this through, the power is actually not in the tongue either. The power is in the mind that controls and tells the tongue what to say. "*Who can tame the tongue?*" (James 3:8). A masterful mind tames the tongue!

So, life and death are in the power of the mind. Yet, if we look a little more deeply, the mind is actually a servant of the matrix, the filters, the theological framework and sociological grid-work that all discriminate, decide and deliver what gets to the mind and how. Matrixes like education, experience and exposure. Filters like culture, country and class. All of this unseen force-field decides how and what information gets to the mind. Finally, we arrive at the matrix, the origin… "*Death and life are in the power of the matrix, that filters information to the mind, that controls the mouth.*" Our mission, as awakened spirits, is two-fold. First, we must be aware of this matrix, mind, mouth, manifestation connection. And, that our lives, or manifestations, are directly connected to how we process information and then choose to declare it. Second, we must ask the Holy Spirit to remove the filters, take away the biases, delete the prejudices, extract the religious leanings and cultural learnings so we can perceive neutrally, purely, clearly and cleanly whatever the Holy Spirit sends to us. This way, we are not merely manifesting with our mouths, minds and matrixes, more separation and segregation into the global human family.

Prayer: *"Master, I surrender my matrix, mind, mouth and manifestation to You. Amen."*

 December 22, 2021

Christ Outside of Christianity

Affirmation

> *"Today, I am awake to the truth that God is omnipresent everywhere and evenly present in all of creation. I am willing to see Christ in all of creation, even outside of Christianity. I am aware that Christ cannot be defined by, nor confined to, any religion. I embrace my interconnectedness with all people and I am surrendered to the idea that in Christ, there is no separation!"*

I often ask people, "What was the difference between Mahatma Gandhi's Civil Rights work in India and South Africa and in Martin Luther King, Jr's Civil Rights Movement in America?" Usually, people agree that both men, and both movements, were very similar. And, even have an awareness that Martin Luther King, Jr. met with and then patterned the American Civil Rights Movement after Gandhi's non-violent resistance philosophies and strategies. Then I ask, "What spirit was working in Martin Luther King, Jr. guiding him to create change?" The answer is always the same…the Spirit of Christ. Then I ask, "What spirit was guiding Gandhi in his work?" Then comes the predictable, expected and confused pauses. And, then the answers, "I don't know?" "Maybe an evil spirit?" "some false Hindu god?" It is very difficult for people to recognize that the same spirit was working in both men, and that they just called it something different.

Interestingly enough, Gandhi was a Jesus fan. Gandhi actually said on one occasion, "I love your Christ…and will encourage all Hindus to follow His teachings on the kingdom of God…I just don't like your Christians. They are not like your Christ." Very telling. In this same vein, Jesus said to His disciples, *"I have sheep of other pastures that you don't know about"* (John 10:16). All of these sheep don't say the sinner's prayer and confess Jesus as their savior. However, the Spirit of Christ is undeniably, recognizably, obviously resident within them. Be willing to see Christ in others, in all of creation and outside of Christianity and religion altogether.

> ***Prayer:*** *"Omnipresent Spirit, I give thanks that You are evenly present in all of creation. I am open to seeing You everywhere. Amen."*

Rock 'n' Roll Jesus

Affirmation

"Jesus is Love. And, love is undeniable and magnetic. People of all ages, colors, countries and cultures are attracted by love. Love also crosses the boundaries of sacred and secular. No matter where you go, Jesus is Just Alright with most people."

You might not think Jesus and Rock 'n' Roll are synonymous. However, you can't listen to rock music for very long without running into lyrics and admiration for Jesus. Lenny Kravitz, singing about Jesus asked *"Are You Gonna Go My Way?"* U2 dedicated the music and lyrics of *"Pride"* to the love of Jesus. The Commodores made it plain that *"Jesus is Love."* Evanescence asked if they could go too far to be saved by Christ in *"Tourniquet."* The Doobie Brothers weren't ashamed to tell the world that *"Jesus Is Just Alright."* Carrie Underwood surrendered and let *"Jesus Take The Wheel."* Kanye West admitted he could only make it because *"Jesus Walks"* with him. Andrew Lloyd Webber wrote an entire musical, *"Jesus Christ Superstar,"* spotlighting Jesus and His teachings. John Legend recently played the role of Jesus in Webber's timeless rock opera on live television Easter Sunday night. I could reference hundreds of secular rock, pop, country, rhythm and blues and hip-hop songs speaking about the love of Jesus and artist's attraction to, and admiration of, Jesus.

Jesus spoke a mystery one day regarding music and the secular marketplace. He said, *"But to what shall I liken this generation? It is like children sitting in the marketplaces and calling to their companions, and saying: 'We played the flute for you, And you did not dance; We mourned to you, but you would not lament."* (Matthew 11:16-17). Jesus described His generation as children playing music in the marketplaces and crying out without much sympathy or response from the religious order. Not much has changed. Rock 'n' Roll holds a special place for Jesus. Always has.

Prayer: *"Rock of Ages, I wanna go Your way, take the wheel, walk with me, You will always be just alright with me. Amen."*

 December 24, 2021

Walk A Mile In My Shoes

Affirmation

"Today, I will endeavor to see life through someone else's eyes. I will dig beneath the surface of inappropriate behaviors and be open see down into root causes. I will resist the urge to become critical or judgmental. And, I will ask the Holy Spirit for wisdom in how to seek out non-threatening ways to lighten someone's heavy burdens."

In the 1970's Joe South wrote a song entitled, *"Walk A Mile In My Shoes."* Consider just a few of the words: *"If I could be you, if you could be me, for just one hour. If we could find a way, to get inside each other's mind. If you could see you through my eyes, instead your own ego. I believe you'd be surprised to see, that you've been blind. Walk a mile in my shoes. Before you abuse, criticize and accuse. Walk a mile in my shoes."*

Is this even possible? To really understand what another person is going through? Perhaps the best we can do is want to understand and maybe relate it to something similar in our own lives…even if it's not an exact parallel. I consider myself to be a compassionate person. One thing that really angers me is animal cruelty. Mistreating or neglecting a harmless animal is beyond me. But, in my journey I have come to grips with the truth that hurting people hurt people, and sometimes animals. The question came to me one day, "What has a human endured to lower them to animalistic, abusive, cruel behavior?" I donate to the ASPCA and Humane Society. And, I treat my dogs like human beings (they sleep in my bed). What causes me to treat an animal like a human? What causes a human to abuse an animal? And, what causes a human to treat another human like an animal? With broader vision, what have people with inappropriate behavior endured on their journeys? Jesus presented the Pharisees with a difficult challenge, *"If you are without sin, cast the first stone."* In other words, before you abuse, criticize and accuse…walk a mile in their shoes.

Prayer: *"God of Compassion, help me see past behavior and into hurt, past the surface and to the root, to walk a mile in another's shoes. Amen."*

December 25, 2021

My Triumphal Entry

Affirmation

"Just as Jesus woke up to His divinity, I am waking up to mine. Today, I will behold the glory of God in the mirror. Today, I will unlock the mystery that the same Spirit that raised Christ from the dead is living in me. Today, I will remember I am created in the image and likeness of God and good. Today, is my Triumphal Entry."

For whatever reason, Jesus forgot that He was divine. He told a young lawyer that He was not good, and not God (Luke 18:19). We can only speculate that perhaps it was to fully identify with the human condition and to feel all we experience in our temporary amnesia to our own divinity? Or maybe He had to mentally be fully man for a season and then wake up to being fully God in order to show us that we carry the same potential of waking up? And still, maybe He actually knew He was divine but hid it for His own safety? No one can be certain. What we do know is that when He rode into Jerusalem, in the Triumphal Entry and what we call Palm Sunday, He was ready to declare His goodness and at was peace with His God-ness.

I love Palm Sunday. The music, the joy, the palms (especially the broken ones…I feel great joy watching the children try to trade their broken palm branches for their friend's unbroken ones). Yet, Palm Sunday is not about the palms, the praise or the people. Palm Sunday is the Triumphal Entry, the moment when Jesus accepted His own divinity personally, privately and publicly. What is your Triumphal Entry? Or better, when is it? It is a joyous day when we realize we are not fallen, hopeless, helpless or wretches saved by grace. When we "*turn*" from Moses (religious bondage) and "*to the Lord*" (Christ Mind) we experience a new "*liberty*." The liberty to "*behold in the mirror the glory of God*" (2 Corinthians 3:16-18). You are divine. Made by God. Made like God. It's personal, accept it privately and then declare it publicly. Let today be your Triumphal Entry.

Prayer: "*God of Awakening and Remembrance, help me to awaken from this sleep and triumph over this amnesia. I am ready. Amen.*"

 December 26, 2021

The Eternal Me

Affirmation

"I am eternal. I was alive before I was born. I will live after my body dies. Today, I will reconnect with the Eternal Me as I resist being burdened by time or bound by any temporary label of race, gender or religion. I will upgrade my thoughts and focus on eternal ideas. I am skinless, sinless, endless, immortal, immutable, immeasurable and unmistakably an eternal spirit having a temporary human experience and expression."

When the young prophet Jeremiah was struggling with insecurity, instability and insignificance, God spoke to him: *"Before I formed you in the womb I knew you; Before you were born I sanctified you; I ordained you a prophet to the nations"* (Jeremiah 1:5).

In other words, God let's Jeremiah know that before his spirit took on physical form it was alive, known, sanctified and ordained. That's quite a bit of pre-incarnate activity before he showed up in his mother's womb. The First Law of Thermodynamics reminds us *"energy can neither be created nor destroyed."* The Hindu holy book The Bhagavad Gita enlightens us *"All that lives, lives forever. Only the shell, the perishable passes away. The spirit is without end. Eternal. Deathless."* The shell carrying Elijah's spirit was taken from the earth. But, that spirit showed back up in the shell called John the Baptist. Jesus said, *"For all the prophets and the law prophesied until John. And if you are willing to receive it, he is Elijah who is to come" (Matthew 11:13-14).* Your spirit is eternal. You were alive before you were born. You will live after your body dies *("to be absent from the body is to be present with the Lord"* 2 Corinthians 5:6). So, don't align with or allow your eternal self to be limited by temporary labels of race or time-laden leashes of religion. This idea terrifies many church leaders because it diminishes the power of hell and defies its doctrines that want us to believe we only have one shot to get it right. You are externally fading, internally unfolding and eternally being. Rebuke time. Refuse temporary. Receive eternity.

Prayer: *"Timeless Truth, I am surrendered to the Eternal Me. Amen."*

December 27, 2021

Get the Devil out of Your Mind and out of Your Mouth

Affirmation

"I no longer need the devil because I am done with blaming others for my life experience. I choose to eat from the Tree of Life and refuse the fruit of the knowledge of good and evil. Today I affirm there is only One Power in the universe. And, that Power is working in, through, as and for me."

"The devil made me do it." No phrase has lulled and kept more people asleep to their power in the history of mankind. Having the devil to blame is a luxury feature that keeps us completely comfortable and incapable of seeing that we are the only devil to blame. Blame is a power thief. And, blaming the devil for what we do takes more of our power than we know. I have had the unfortunate experience of being around intoxicated individuals who behave poorly. Then, later on, in a sober state, blame their inappropriate actions on the alcohol. The alcohol is not to be blamed. The alcohol just provides an excuse to do what you want to do sober, but don't have the nerve or an excuse. Many Christians are drunk on the devil, blaming him for all of their poor choices and bad behavior.

I am not sure I just stopped believing in the devil one day. I feel like I just realized I didn't need the devil anymore and the devil just kind of faded away. I like to say, "Get the devil out of your mind and out of your mouth, and the devil will get out of your life." Or, from the words of Jesus, "*make no place for the devil and he will flee.*" There doesn't have to be an official exorcism or even a rebuking of the devil. Just simply make no place for the devil by not needing him or anything else to blame. You will never truly have power until you realize there is only One Power in the universe. And, that Power is not separate from you. When we praise God for the good and blame the devil for the bad, we subtly and subconsciously continue to eat from the Tree of the Knowledge of Good and Evil. It's all God. Humanity's misuse of its divine creativity can at times certainly seem like the devil. Yet, it's only a lack of navigating our divine creativity. Keep your power. Hone your power. Own your power. And, watch the devil flee.

Prayer: *"Strong Deliverer, today I will make no place for the devil. Amen."*

12/28/2021

Awake to my Time, Task, Treasure and Temple

Affirmation

"Today, I intend to be fully awake to my time, my task, my treasure and my temple. I am aware that when I am on time I am inviting money and people with money into my life. When I am on task and prepared I am declaring to the universe that I am available for opportunities and success. When I manage my treasure wisely I am opening a portal for more to arrive. And, when I am awake to my body temple I am laying a foundation for a long, healthy life."

In Luke chapter 19, Jesus teaches the importance of being a good steward over very little. The reward for this stewardship is to be trusted with more. I am not sure there is an exact science for finding success and welcoming money into our lives. But, being on time, showing up prepared for our task, making responsible decisions with our treasure and respecting our body temples are huge steps in the right direction. Obviously, these four areas all begin with the letter "T." There is one "T" word that is missing here that many people believe is the key to success. But, I have actually found that, although it may be helpful, it is not always necessary and sometimes can even be a hindrance to success. That "T" word is…Talent.

I have been around fabulously talented athletes, musicians, speakers, entrepreneurs and creative minds my entire life. Generally, the more talented a person is, the less they are on time, the less prepared they are when they show up late, the less they manage their money when they make it and the less they respect their body temple by feeding it, exercising it and resting it properly. Talent seems to be the most detrimental piece to managing time, task, treasure and temple. The great ones, who enjoy a long life full of money, opportunities, health and happiness are the ones who can mix in their God-given talent with their time, task, treasure and temple. Welcome a lifetime of success today by being faithful over little things. And watch, as God blesses you with more.

Prayer: *"Source of Blessings, as I am faithful over little I know You will trust me with more. Amen."*

Victim of Chance? Or Agent of Change?

Affirmation

"I am not a human victim of chance. I am a divine agent of change. I am not the things that happened to me. I am what I do with the things that happened to me. I am not the names people have called me. I am only what I answer to. And today, my name is not victim. My name is victory."

In a counseling session years ago, I sat with a middle-aged individual who was heavily burdened with painful memories from their childhood and the neglect from their father. They explained how the lack of fatherly love was now affecting their ability to be affectionate with their spouse and their own children. Tears, tantrums and a lot of tissue later, I finally suggested that this person needed closure and should go to their father and express how the neglect had affected their life. The individual then paused from the emotional outburst and said, "I can't do that. My father has been dead for twenty-five years." I was stunned that this level of emotional pain was still present all these years later. I said to this person, "A man who has been in the grave twenty-five years is still running and ruining your life?" This seemed to strike a chord and bring about an awakening that enough was enough. The individual said to me, "Why should I allow a person who is dead to destroy the life and good years I have left?"

All of us carry painful memories and images from our childhood. Some people believe we chose to come here and even chose our parents and families. Whether we choose our parents or it is all a game of chance, we can create purposeful change that provides us with a life full of love and joy. Pain unreleased and unresolved can be passed down for generations. Don't allow chance to run and ruin your life. Be a change agent. If your parents were neglectful, be the change in your kid's lives. If you grew up without love, be the change and give love. You will find that when you give out of the place of your pain you will experience a powerful sense of healing knowing that what may have happened to you by chance is now the fuel empowering you to create change.

Prayer: *"Divine Change Agent, help me be the change today. Amen."*

Father, Forgive Them...They Know Not

Affirmation

"I absolve you of any guilt or wrongdoing. I know you were doing the best you could with the information you had. This is not to say you had the right information or to say that what you did to me was justifiable in any way. However, peace is ordained in my life and the order of the day. And today, you and I are at peace. I release you into your next season free from any guilt or obligation. And, I pray for your happiness and well-being."

How would our lives be radically changed if we could say these words to those who have hurt us? Even if the words aren't uttered audibly, saying these words within our own hearts and minds could spark a mental restoration and begin an emotional healing that would welcome a sense of peace and closure that we have longed for. Notice, we are not saying what happened was right. We are not even saying we understand or sympathize. We are acknowledging that people who know better, do better. And, people who do not know better, do not do better.

In this framework, consider the words of Jesus as He was dying on the cross, *"Father, forgive them. They don't know what they are doing."* Like Jesus, we can forgive ignorance, and the hurt it inflicts upon us, without agreeing that the ignorance is accurate. It is entirely possible to forgive family ignorance, to protect our children from it, and to live in a higher realm of conscious awareness, without ever promoting it or passing it on to future generations. The hurt was and is real. Bad things do happen to us at the hands of ignorant people. Yet, give thanks! What didn't kill us only made us stronger. We have learned the power of forgiveness. And, we have realized that we do not share the same ignorance of those who hurt us because of theirs. We know better. We can now do better. Choose forgiveness. Cherish peace. Channel freedom.

Prayer: *"Merciful Father, today I give thanks that You have helped me survive ignorance, forgive it, heal from it and learn from it. Amen."*

Nurse, Curse, Rehearse, Reverse

Affirmation

"I recognize that I have been betrayed, lied about, falsely accused, rejected, abandoned, hurt and have experienced pain throughout my life. I am also aware that I cannot live in this hurt forever or allow this pain to become a filter through which I see and create life. Today, I make the conscious decision not to Nurse It, Curse It, or Rehearse It, and I know God will Reverse It."

Today, our 100th and last affirmation, involves a subject that will require a little more time as we are going to dissect a very powerful biblical story together. Our last day is going to be longer than any other day. But, it will be worth it. And, it will be a final moment of clarity and mental healing for all of us.

The three Hebrew children (Shadrach, Meshach and Abed-Nego) are in a situation where the king (Nebuchadnezzar) is attempting to force them to worship his god, his way. The three Hebrew children refuse and it angers the king. The king decides to put them to death in a fiery furnace. Let's walk through this process as we learn the valuable lesson not to Nurse It, Curse It, or Rehearse It, and then watch God Reverse It.

> *"He spoke and commanded that they heat the furnace seven times more than it was usually heated. And he commanded certain mighty men of valor who were in his army to bind Shadrach, Meshach, and Abed-Nego, and cast them into the burning fiery furnace"* (Daniel 3:19-20).

Notice here, the king orders the furnace to be heated 7 times hotter than normal. In biblical symbology, 7 is always a day of completion and rest, meaning, this furnace is not designed to kill them. This situation is designed to perfect them. Also, be aware that the soldiers who put them into the furnace, at the king's command, were *"mighty men of valor."* This will be important later.

"Then these men were bound in their coats, their trousers, their turbans, and their other garments, and were cast into the midst of the burning fiery furnace" (Daniel 3:21).

The important piece here is that the three Hebrew children went into the fire bound. But, they are about to come out free.

"...the flame of the fire killed those men who took up Shadrach, Meshach, and Abed-Nego" (Daniel 3:22).

Remember the *"mighty men of valor"* who put the three Hebrew children into the furnace? The fire actually killed them. So, we can see two aspects of wisdom here. One, when people set traps for you, be at peace. When you keep your mind right and spirit free from lower thinking, the trap they set for you will actually ensnare them. Second, these seemingly good, trustworthy, powerful men of valor, entered into the king's offense. Yet, the king survived this situation while they were killed. The lesson is this: Don't enter into other people's hurts. We are here to heal the room, to help people grow past their hurts, not to enter into their offenses with them.

"Look!" he answered, "I see four men loose, walking in the midst of the fire; and they are not hurt, and the form of the fourth is like the Son of God" (Daniel 3:25).

Because of their attitude in this difficult situation, the three Hebrew children are not hurt by this unfair and unjust situation. They went in bound. They came out free from bondage. And, in the midst of their most trying time, there is a fourth Man in the fire, who looks like the Son of God! We are never alone in painful moments. We can confidently rest in the knowledge that in the darkest seasons of our lives, the Spirit of Christ walks with us.

"...on whose bodies the fire had no power; the hair of their head was not singed nor were their garments affected, and the smell of fire was not on them" (Daniel 3:27).

Wow! This heated situation has not harmed them. Their bodies, their possessions, and most importantly, their spirits, are not affected. The smell of fire or smoke was not on them. So many times, I have witnessed people survive very stressful, trying, unfair and painful seasons. Survive is an accurate word because they smell like a survivor. The pain, the anger, the bitterness all seem to be a lingering stink they wear for the rest of their lives. When you come out…let it go…let God…laugh, love, live…and forgive. Refuse to smell like pain. Resist the stink of bitterness. Reject the stench of anger. And, receive the reward of righteousness, peace and joy!

"Then the king promoted Shadrach, Meshach, and Abed-Nego in the province of Babylon" (Daniel 3:30).

This story ends with Shadrach, Meshach and Abed-Nego being promoted in a strange land, finding favor with the king who tried to destroy them and influencing the king to have a new openness to their way of connecting with God. When we maintain a high vibration, even in moments of stress and strain, we influence people's lives for good, and for God. And, even turn enemies into allies..

> ***Prayer:*** *"Fourth Man in the Fire, thank You for walking with me and for delivering me out of the fires that were designed to destroy me. Help me to not smell like smoke, or the pain of my past, for one more day. Allow my example of love, openness and forgiveness to bring peace to volatile situations. As I keep my peace, I trust You to defend me and promote me. Today, I will not Nurse It, Curse It, or Rehearse It. And, I will watch as You Reverse It! Amen."*

Keep reading for a preview of D.E. Paulk's book and manual for rethinking the Bible:

The Holy Bible of Inclusion

SECOND EDITION

If you are like me you have struggled to accept the modern Christian church's portrayal (or betrayal) of God, depiction of the devil and description of hell. Many god-fearing people and good-hearted preachers alike have long harbored unspoken thoughts of a more loving, merciful and masterful Creator. However, just about as many who subscribe to this grander vision and version of God also admittedly and even ashamedly lack the ability to reference the Bible and specific passages of scripture in order to publicly validate these privately held higher concepts of God.

If you are looking for *chapter and verse* that will both quickly and completely rescue a big God from the smallness of fundamentalism, *THE HOLY BIBLE OF INCLUSION* is precisely the tool you need! *THE HOLY BIBLE OF INCLUSION* will scripturally, extensively and even exhaustively confront theological myths, misrepresentations and mistranslations of *the Bible and its Origins – Universal Salvation – the devil – the Purpose of hell and the Fire of God – Sexual Orientation* and many others. Join me on this worthwhile and rewarding spiritual journey as we research, rethink, recover and then re-present the awesome and awe-inspiring God of the universe.

Who is going to harm you if you are eager to do good? But even if you should suffer for what is right, you are blessed. "Do not fear their threats; do not be frightened." But in your hearts revere Christ as Lord. ***ALWAYS BE PREPARED TO GIVE AN ANSWER TO EVERYONE WHO ASKS YOU TO GIVE A REASON FOR THE HOPE THAT YOU HAVE.*** *But do this with gentleness and respect, keeping a clear conscience, so that those who speak maliciously against your good behavior in Christ may be ashamed of their slander. For it is better, if it is God's will, to suffer for doing good than for doing evil. For Christ also suffered once for sins, the righteous for the unrighteous, to bring you to God.*

I Peter 3:13-18 NIV

Second Edition Update from the Author...

What is the survivability of inclusive religion? This was the question haunting me when I first published The Holy Bible of Inclusion in 2010. Specifically, how do you transition a traditional, Evangelical Christian church into expressions of LGBTQ+ affirmation, universal salvation and interfaith oneness / openness without losing the church? Pragmatically, can a church shift in thought and still pay the bills?

Current scholarship and pew research reveal that American Christians are opening to a greater sense of inclusivity while more than 20% of Americans who formerly identified as Christian no longer wish to be identified with any single religion. However, problematically this shift in theological opinion is mostly held in a scared space of secret devotion. This awakening to inclusion seems to be trapped in personal journey, encountering a number of roadblocks when attempting to manifest itself openly in American church settings. Can individual, personal leanings toward inclusion, pluralism, and LGBTQ+ affirmation survive the transition from private spiritual ascension to public articulation and systematic actualization? Can these personal, individual "aha" moments emerge into corporate church modality? I believe they can. And, as a pastor who has successfully transitioned a traditional Pentecostal Christian church into a more inclusive, even pluralistic expression, I speak from experience…this shift is possible! However, knowing how to "rightly divide the Word of truth" is the key to survival.

Christians do not speak English. They speak Christianese, or better, the King James Version of Christianese. What does this mean? In order to survive the shift from tradition to inclusion, you have to know the Word of God and then be able to explain it in a nuanced way that satisfies those who have been conditioned to worship it. I wrote this book to save my church over a decade ago. Many were ready to walk out the door at the time of this book's arrival. As we investigated hundreds of scriptures justifying inclusive expression, many turned around, sat back down, and are still with me today.

This is my exhortation to you: If you know God is bigger than any religion or human construct, and want to survive the transition from private thought to public expression - study this book, salvage your church, save your marriage, secure your family and friendships, and "show it to them in the Word" - all from your deep knowledge of the Bible!

Fully Awake,

D. E.

Then He opened their minds so they could
understand the Scriptures.
Luke 24:45 – NIV

In his book, *THE HOLY BIBLE OF INCLUSION*, Pastor D. E. Paulk does a much more thorough and comprehensive job of probing the critical concepts of *Inclusion* than I do in my book, *THE GOSPEL OF INCLUSION.* The delicate theological, scriptural and spiritual balance my friend D. E. Paulk walks and writes in this book, is an artistic, tactful and tasteful treatment of some of the most sensitive aspects of both modern and ancient religious doctrine, dogma and discipline.

The subject of *Inclusion* deals more with being and feeling spiritually and mentally *safe* than being and feeling religiously *saved.* I am proud of the expanded consciousness this book embraces and embarks upon in further discussion. During this journey you will inevitably enjoy renewing and re-knowing God (and yourself) all over again - or perhaps for the first time.

Peace is possible.

~ Bishop Carlton D. Pearson

THE HOLY BIBLE OF INCLUSION
CONTENTS

INVITATION OF TRUTH

As we journey through the Word of God together, searching for hidden truths that have remained concealed for many years, we must invite the Spirit of God to guide us into TRUTH. If you are in agreement, read aloud this simple Invitation of Truth:

My mind is alert and my Spirit is open to receive Truth. I acknowledge that Truth is not reserved only to what I already know and is not merely restricted to concepts with which I am already familiar. As beauty is in the eye of the beholder – Truth is in the ear, heart and mind of the perceiver.

INTRODUCTION

I could say "the glass is half full" and then say of the same glass that it is also "half empty" – and each of these opposing statements would be strangely true, correct, accurate. It is true. The same glass that is half full is also half empty. Both of these statements are "right." Whether we see the glass half full or half empty does not reveal accuracy or correctness or rightness about the water or the glass. How we view the glass only brings to light our personal perspective and level of consciousness.

In many Christian circles, there has been much theological debate around the doctrine of *Universal Salvation*. Other "less threatening" offshoot names associated with Universal Salvation are: *Ultimate Reconciliation*, the *Finished Work of Grace* and the *Restoration of All Things*. However, *INCLUSION* is the name (at least for the past decade) that has received the greater majority of attention. From an exhaustive, thorough study of the scriptures (including both Old and New Testaments) – we can, and will, accurately prove that Universal Salvation is an original, sound and recurring doctrine throughout the whole Bible. Yet, we also find a consistent biblical pattern that would line up with a more fundamentalist or evangelical expression and interpretation.

So, how do we choose?

Which Bible do we read?

The Universal, Progressive, *Inclusive* Bible?

The Fundamentalist, Evangelical, *Exclusive* Bible?

The Bible is a holy book (or a collection of 66 holy books) containing contrasting (even contradicting) truths. And, it is designed that way. The contradictions are there intentionally to encourage growth and a greater depth of understanding. They are meant to catapult us into higher revelations. The Bible is a progression of man's process of wrestling with the unending truth of an eternal God. The Bible is a beautiful story of humanity's struggle and surrender to becoming divine. And, along this journey we utilize the Bible, not to declare or prove specific doctrines as absolute truth – but, we corporately use the Bible as a mirror to show us where we are individually on the path to enlightenment. If the Bible contains purposeful contradicting truths…then the Bible we choose to read (whether inclusive or exclusive) only reveals our personal level of spiritual growth and our degree of awakened consciousness.

In the final analysis, this "argument" has proven to be counterproductive to achieving a cohesive collaboration and a closer common union in the greater Body of Christ. As long as the ultimate goal, from either viewpoint, is to prove someone or something to be right or wrong (the glass to be half full or half empty) we will never see the beauty and necessity of celebrating a diversity of expression and function in the same Body.

Inevitably, when theological arguments ensue, people become polarized to one position or the other, allowing very little room for open-minded discussion, thus effectively preventing any possibility of learning anything from someone who may have a perspective other than their own. As a fourth generation preacher, I have seen my share of doctrinal schism, and have heard of even more. Biblical argument is just about as old as the Bible itself. And, Christianity is an extremely scripture-driven religion. Someone who has been raised with the Bible as if it were a long-standing trusted family member will usually not even give consideration to an unfamiliar spiritual concept without first being shown some sort of foundational scriptural reference or evidence. If I had a dime for every time I have heard someone say – "Show it to me in the Word" – I would… well, have a lot of dimes.

Keep reading for a preview of D.E. Paulk's book and journey toward surrender, self-awareness and the evolution of consciousness:

I DON'T KNOW...

the way of

KNOWING

SECOND EDITION

I Don't Know is the required confession needed to be granted admission to the path of enlightenment and to The Way of Knowing. I Know is conclusive, ending, finite and therefore devastating. I Know is an enemy of immortality and nemesis to The Way of Knowing. We are all infinite spirits and the offspring of the Infinite Creator. When we discover the I Don't Know within we unleash our Infinite nature and unearth the Endless Us! Are you ready to put on immortality?

All Truth flows to us from One Divine River. From that One River many wells form and are fed. We might call these wells religions, cultures or philosophies. All wells sustained by the One River contain beauty and truth. However, we make a grave mistake when we declare any particular well as being the One River. I Don't Know dissolves religious division, bridges cultural chasms and dodges philosophical divorce originating from the I Know. I Don't Know is the Repairer of the Breach. In a day when the I Know is to be charged with so much human suffering - I Don't Know shines brightly as an ancient idea whose time has come of age.

Foreword

Dr. Carlton Pearson

Knowledge is both the most intriguing and most ambiguous of realities. It is and isn't; simultaneously. I am actually, for the first time in my life, more curious about what I don't know than what I believe. I think we all believe too much and know too little.

What you know, what you think, what you feel and what you believe are all interrelated, but not equal. The combination of all of them facilitates *Being*. The segregation of them facilitates the dysfunctionalism and desperation we see all around us.

I believe that authentic truth is not so much learned or taught, but remembered. It is more recovery than discovery. In the deepest recesses of our individual souls, we know everything, because we *are* everything. God made us this way. We were created in the image and likeness of Divinity. This would be Divinity with us, in us, for us and ultimately as us!

In some ways, knowledge and knowing might be different. Knowledge is usually based on information while *knowing* is based on transformation. One is based on fact the other on faith, which is inner persuasion. It is less external and lives both internally and eternally with and as us.

As I am now over half a century old, for the first time in my life I feel as if *being* has more essence and more importance than knowing, after all we are called human *beings,* not human doings or even knowings. Both are part of our *Being*, but in many ways we've neglected being, choosing knowing and doing over being. Being is our first and foremost Self. Knowing and doing come out of Being, but if Being is ignored, negated or neglected, knowing and doing become counter-productive and imprecise. It is this inaccuracy of emphasis that causes most of the pain and pathos of human disease and/or dis-ease.

I studied five and a half years in university seeking knowledge, but while doing so, my *Being* was shrinking and shriveling because that's the only way it could fit in the smaller garments and wardrobe of knowledge.

I majored in Biblical Literature/English Bible and minored in Theology and Historical Studies. I know the history, but I am, in my being, *the mystery.* Being is both who you are and who you are not, the part of you that is and is not. It is both sides of YOU-ness or YOU-niverse!

Being doesn't need clothes. It is the truest, purest and original form of nakedness. It is the nakedness Adam and Eve (the male and female in us all and that we all indeed are) had before they felt shame. The only darkness there is the Light you are and aren't... Selah!

The shame and sham religious pre-supposition can be is what robs us of our sense of being and prevents us from knowing, beyond knowledge acquisition. Institutionalized religion fills us with knowledge of the doctrines, disciplines and dogmas that pervade human culture worldwide and often cause and then activate the war of the worlds. This knowledge often hinders and hampers "Knowing" which is the essence of being, who we are and are becoming.

The sense of self and soul is what I call *Self Actualization.* Learning, or should I say, remembering to be actually, factually, functionally and punctually <u>YOU</u> is what *being* really is.

Pastor D. E. Paulk, my friend and colleague in ministry, has tackled an issue few even acknowledge exists. The over certitude of many and most of the world religions have kept us from accessing, experiencing, expanding and expressing the greatest of the ethereal disciplines, the discipline of *Not Knowing* and being at peace with, and actually becoming, one with the *Unknown.* Anything else is probably an illusion!

I pride my self in not knowing anything except that I know little… but remain open and eager to know more, which means essentially, to know ME. Knowing you is being you. Being you is experiencing God! And for most of us, Knowing begins with the simple admission – *I Don't Know.*

Second Edition Update From The Author

D.E. Paulk

When I first published I DON'T KNOW…The Way Of Knowing in 2008, I had not been introduced to the wisdom traditions of Zen bardo space, Buddhist emptiness, Beginner's Mind, or to the Judaic, Kabbalistic Chabad ideal of celebrating nothingness. I knew Jesus. I had studied the Gospels my entire life. But, I had not yet seen the mystical Christ. In my desire for mastery of doctrine, I had not allowed myself to become "like a child" to enter the Kingdom. My entire life I had "heard of old" but was not hearing what Spirit was saying. I had not yet begun to celebrate the not-knowingness resident within Jesus, who explains that the children of the Kingdom are "like the wind…blowing here and there…no one knowing where it comes from or to where it is going."

I just said these three simple words, "I DON'T KNOW!" All of a sudden the knowING began to flow to me, through me, and most importantly, from within me. Whatever was necessary for the evolution of my consciousness began to show up. Somehow I had opened a portal to the wisdom of the Universe, not by way of reading or research, but by removing the obstacles of presupposition, conditioning and the know-it-all-ness that had kept the knowING from awakening within me.

Eventually, I stumbled upon Taoist ideas like "When the student is ready, the Teacher will appear." Lao Tzu showed up and reminded me that "knowing, without knowing, was true enlightenment." But, at the time of my awakening, I only knew I had surrendered what I thought I knew in my hunger to know more. Since that time, I have found that truth is a journey, not a destination. I have realized that I am not my beliefs, but the spirit capable of having, changing and considering beliefs. I have detached from any false identity of being my mind and have surrendered to the idea that I am not my thoughts, or even the thinker of thoughts, but the observer of the thinker having thoughts. It is from this approach that the Holy Spirit is granted complete permission to guide into all truth. It is in this methodology, not in a specific doctrine or truth, where safeguards against spiritual stagnation and mental constipation can be realized.

If you are reading this book in quest for specific truths or concrete answers, you will end up dissatisfied. Religion tells us what to think. But, spirituality teaches us how to think. This book is not designed to teach you anything. It is designed to remove the obstacles that keep you from seeing what you already know. Or rather, to teach you how to think and provide an approach that will open an eternal channel where truth(s) are always available. You are neither destined to get stuck on a specific truth nor fated to be tied to a specific teacher - "When the student is truly ready, the Teacher will disappear."

The fifth word in the Bible is "created" (Genesis 1:1- "in the beginning God created"). Created in Hebrew is bara – which means to "carve away" or "clear out space." In essence, when God was creating the earth, God was actually re-creating the earth. God was carving away and clearing out space in order for something else to emerge. As we begin this creative journey, find some available space for God to create. I offer this affirmation as a temporary guide, leading us to the emptiness that fills us, to the nothingness that is the all-ness and to the knowledge of not knowing:

"I am not my thoughts. I am not the thinker of my thoughts. I am the observer, witnessing the thinker, thinking the thoughts. I am not the voice in my head or any limitation of an inherited collective cultural conditioning, religious indoctrination or even my past experiences. Wisdom of the ages and sages, grant me the surrender to mind my mind, free my mind, be free of my mind and surrender to practice no-mind."

There is nothing better than to know that you don't know.
Not knowing, yet thinking you know, this is sickness.
- Lao Tzu